BAND
- A Philsophy

Richard Graham

Copyright © 2021 Richard Graham
All rights reserved.
ISBN: 978-1-5272-9656-5

To none but God
To nothing but the glory of God

Contents

Introduction	1
B A N D	
Part 1: Both and Neither	
Chapter 1: Who Am I? What Am I?	13
Chapter 2: "Where Are You From?"	18
Chapter 3: Self Revolution	32
Chapter 4: Self Resolution	46
Chapter 5: Towards A New World	55
Chapter 6: Tips and Takeaways	63
Part 2: Banned from Belonging	
Chapter 7: Why Am I? Where Am I?	71
Chapter 8: Politics	85
Chapter 9: School	100
Chapter 10: Work, i.e. "Jobs"	115
Chapter 11: Religion	128
Chapter 12: In Conclusion	141
Part 3: Band Together	
Chapter 13: When Am I? How Am I?	163
Part 4: Love	
Chapter 14: God	183

Introduction

Thank you.

    Before anything and everything—thank you, and welcome. Thank you for being alive. Thank you for making it this far. Thank you for picking up this book, for opening the pages, and for reading these words. Welcome.
    You might be thinking: Why the gratitude? Personally, I'm not a big believer in coincidences; it may certainly be a stretch to say that everything in life is "meant to be" and predetermined (if that's the case, then whatever does the determining sure does fit in a lot of trivialities!), but I do believe—or rather, I know—that some aspects, the key moments, are intended and imbued with a deeper purpose. Such a statement is perhaps anathema to the modern mind, which demands measurable evidence and logical, rational proof for all beliefs, or to the champions of uninhibited

liberty who reject all ideas alluding to a power beyond their own free will. Indeed, it is not a statement I can, or even care, to prove in a manner that others find acceptable or convincing. For I know that any sense of meaning and purpose behind events is a matter of one's perspective; it is dependent on a mindset of searching, of wanting to see, rather than being told.

Answers are provided if you ask, things are found if you seek, doors are opened if you knock. Whether or not we perceive a deeper or higher cause to the seemingly random occurrences to our lives is contingent on ourselves.

It is, in many respects, a choice.

Insofar that such a choice is not based on observable, verifiable evidence, however, it is considered, in the world in which we live, to be "irrational." To seek meaning or purpose behind various situations and events in our lives and in the world around us is viewed as foolish or even dangerous. We inhabit a world that attempts to sway our freedom—to have us *not* choose to search deeper, or look wider, and instead to simply accept the blur of all that happens around us as coincidental and purposeless. This, to be sure, is the attitude of the reasonable and rational in our time. As they would have it, we would be doing ourselves and everyone else a great favor by sticking to this script, focusing on more realistic matters in the form of the next random event, and understanding it in the way we are told to. In other words, stick your head in the sand, close your eyes, and shut up.

Though if you share such a disposition, I won't ask you to suddenly reorient your worldview, to start piecing together all that has happened in your life and the wider world into one great picture of interconnection and purpose—now *that* would be unrealistic. But what I would ask for, if I may, is an open mind, at least for the duration of time that you have the pages of this book open and are reading its words. It is not my intention to tell you definitively the significance of your life and the meaning of the world we inhabit, if any. That, to say again, is a matter of perspective and choice on your part, and yours alone. However, it is also true that I have written this book to offer my understanding of those matters. If only for the sake of making the best use of the limited, precious time we have together, then, please consider what I offer here, expanding your imagination and asking yourself, "What if"—

What if our lives do have significance and value?

What if there is intention guiding our lives, and the state of our being is not random but rather meant to be?

Indeed, specifically on the latter, could you entertain the possibility that there is not only an active force of goodness—of love—that seeks the best for us, that yearns for nothing and no one but the truth of you and I, but also that there are powers of evil and hatred that attempt to control us, to crush us? Could it be that not only is the beauty, growth, and vitality that we experience in our lives a consequence of intention, but so too the chaos, confusion, and darkness; that these two opposing forces are locked in a titanic struggle—a cosmic war—with our minds as the battleground, and our *spirit* as the ultimate prize?

And most importantly, could you entertain the possibility that it is us who have the power to determine the victor, that the outcome is decided by a choice—*our* choice?

Could it be?

Even if there is only the slightest creaking-open of your mind's door to such possibilities, our time together will, I assure you, be infinitely more valuable and rewarding. And who knows? It might even be that, once we are done, that small breach made to a mind once closed will come to be burst wide open.

So, on that note, again, thank you for choosing to read this book. Welcome. Thank you for all the choices that you made leading up to reading this book, and thank you for being alive. None was a coincidence; all happened for us to be together in this very moment and, indeed, for all that will transpire from this moment forward.

My journey to produce this work has itself been one which very much encourages a perspective of seeing meaning and purpose, almost to the point that to not see would be irrational or even foolish. This has been a project that has tied so many elements of my life together, with ideas and writings that were brought into being at various points in time for no reason other than to express my thoughts on particular occasions, having suddenly been resurrected by relevance and finding a home in the pages before you. Thoughts and notes that were once disjointed and atomized have been engrafted into an entire web of purpose—almost, it would seem, by providence. But more than just past sentiments and writings, I have come to understand this book as the culmination of a long, winding process, very much a lifetime in the making. Disconnected tributaries of my life thus far seem to have coalesced, with their amalgamation creating new form, their unity bringing forth new life. It is a strange sensation indeed, that past experiences that otherwise would be suspended in isolation were all a bridge leading up to this, to now. In a very real sense, I feel as if I was born to do this and to have this moment with you.

To arrive at this point, however, has been far from a painless and leisurely journey. Indeed, quite the opposite, with the inception of this book being driven by an irrepressible feeling of psychological dissatisfaction with a life untrue to who I am and a gnawing sense of spiritual exile within the world in which I am situated. On several occasions have I attempted to snuff out these feelings, to ignore them, to pretend they are of no consequence, in the hope that, one day, they just might evaporate and vanish. But as we sooner or later discover in life, avoiding the elephant in the room never seems to have the effect of making it disappear. So it is in response to these feelings that I have been spurred to write—to address the elephant once and for all and to see what is revealed by the process of confrontation.

Upon recognizing these feelings of discontent within myself, I have also taken the liberty to assume that there must be many, many others who share them. Thus in addition to restorative introspection, this book is also intended as a means to reach out and see for myself whether this is actually the case—to find a community of those who look at themselves and the world, and sense deep within that there is something else, something more; to connect with those who are guided by this inexplicable feeling that has always been there, that stirs a certain yearning and brings together the people who are searching for answers coaxed by it. And, indeed, if you do feel and think the same way, perhaps this book can serve to reassure you that you're not alone and simply going insane—that at least it's the two of us who are out of our minds!

That being said, however, it would be somewhat disingenuous for me to speak of what I have to offer here as something completely out of this world. You may recognize some ideas as being similar to others you have heard before, maybe even from some rather eminent thinkers. Certainly, I have been influenced by several sources that I have encountered throughout my life, whilst I am sure there are a great many with which I have not been in contact but that share similar sentiments. As with all works of this nature, mine has not been born from a black hole in which nothing has been seen or heard; needless to say, therefore, I do not hold any resemblance or correlation with other ideas, deliberate or not, as a compromise to authenticity. If anything, all who have expressed ideas similar to those presented herein are, in my view, my friends. We are a part of the same community, drawing from the same source of self-evident knowledge and arriving at similar conclusions because, well, that's probably just what makes the most sense.

But though this be the case, it is also my hope, of course, that the originality of the work is evident. For although the range of topics covered within are far-reaching and diverse, and the majority not necessarily being "about me," I present this to you as, more than anything, the ultimate act of self-expression. This is a piece born from my idiosyncratic observations on the world we inhabit and the world within myself, with no institutional sponsorship, ideological justification, group ties, or obligations. The hope and intent is for it to serve as a break from my past self and to thereupon build a new world having declared the real *me* and the truth of this person that I am—a truth that, fundamentally, I believe we all share. Thus, with full cognizance of the very real possibility, or rather inevitability, of the social ostracization that will result from "coming clean" in this manner, it is admittedly with some trepidation that I come before you, simply and merely as myself, with all my heart and soul, my entire being etched into the words that follow. Drawing from the late, great W. B. Yeats' *Aedh Wishes for the Cloths of Heaven*, therefore, please try to read what follows slowly, purposefully, and with merciful contemplation—for I have spread my soul unto these words; tread carefully, because you tread on my soul.

For the final time, then, thank you for choosing to read this book. It has been the greatest pleasure and privilege for me to write, and I hope it can do its part in making this world a little less confused, lonely, angry, and divided; that it can contribute to creating a better world, one more closely resembling our innermost dreams and potential.

Most of all, I pray my words can serve to build a bridge—a band—between you and me.

BAND

— Both and Neither
Multiplicity. Identity.

— Banned from Belonging
Conflict. Exile.

— Band Together
Resolution. Unity.

—

Part 1
Both and Neither
Multiplicity. Identity.

Chapter 1
Who Am I? What Am I?

We are all born into this world.

We see the same sky, breathe the same air; we are sustained by the same sun. We all stand on the same ground and wish upon the same stars.

At our most fundamental, you and I—we're the same.

And yet, simultaneously we are each unique. By natural means or otherwise, there never has, is, or will be another you—your existence, your identity, your *spirit*. You and I are the same, and yet we are totally and absolutely unique. Our sameness and difference coexist; our differences do not separate us. We are all the same; we are all unique. We are unique waves of the same sea. Unique leaves of the same tree. Unique rays of light emanating from the same source. Unique points of attention of the same infinity.

It may be that our lives are but a blink of an eye in cosmic terms, and thus our existence may often seem utterly small and insignificant, a speck of dust on the greatest and most massive of surfaces. Yet the total and absolute uniqueness of each one of us dictates that the value of each be total and absolute likewise. There is no better or worse, higher or lower, superior or inferior. To say again, we are all the same; we are all unique. Further, we are unrepeatable, irreplaceable, incalculable, invaluable.

Our difference and uniqueness, as our most treasured asset—our most precious gift—is our greatest contribution to the infinity of human diversity. If there ever was a calling, a mission, a purpose to our lives, it is to live the life of this unique manifestation, this miracle, to its absolute utmost. It is the cultivation of self, the nurturing of *I* to the uttermost degree—indeed, for the higher sake of *us*.

For if we are all unique, each with a particular and exclusive path that none before or after will ever tread, then it is you who must walk this way.

Only I can walk the path of *I*.

So ask yourself: Who am *I*? What am *I*?

What are your answers to those questions? I suppose they could include any number of things: name, nationality, religion, occupation, gender, political affiliation, to name but a few possibilities. But ask yourself this: Why did I answer those questions in the way that I did, or how I would, should they be asked again?

I asked myself the same, and the answer I came to was that my responses are what I define myself by and how I identify as myself. They are the primary ingredients I see as the makeup of me, that which encapsulates my sense of self, of who and what I believe myself to be. Indeed, my answers are the foremost *experiences* that have come to dominate my perception of my identity.

I am (name). I am (nationality). I am (religion). I am (occupation). I am (gender). I am (political affiliation). I am (whatever).

Such aspects are all experiences, and it is by these that we perceive ourselves as "I."

From where did these answers, these experiences, come? We chose them as our respective responses, but who, or what, gave them to us? To ask again: *Why* did we choose to answer those questions in the way that we did, or how we would, should they be asked again? Clearly, some we have chosen and vested upon ourselves. We may have chosen our own name, or chosen to accept the one bestowed to us. Likewise for our nationality, religion, occupation, sexual orientation, political affiliation, or anything else. Some we have chosen for ourselves, others we have received and chosen to accept. Either way, the facets of our response are the product of our choices.

Next, and perhaps the most important question of all: Are you satisfied with those answers? Are you satisfied with who you are, and the experience that is your life as you currently live it? Do your answers accurately and truly describe who you are? Do your answers resemble *you*?

Does your nationality define everywhere you come from? Does your religion define everything you believe to be true? Does your occupation define everything you do? Does your political affiliation define everything you stand for?

To some of these, the answer you provided for yourself might be satisfactory already. If, for instance, you were born in a given country, and both your parents were born in the same country, and you identify solely with that country, then perhaps to state this country as your nationality makes the most sense. Perhaps you are Christian or Buddhist, Capitalist or Communist, and believe in all the things the authorities, texts, codes, commandments, and conventions these respective worldviews and ideologies claim.

In this regard, perhaps there are aspects of our stated identity that we have settled for, certain experiences that we do not question. But for many of us, there will also be areas we are not satisfied with, facets that we feel do not sit quite right with who we instinctively know ourselves to be and that are not a part of who we *actually* are.

I know this to be true, because I was one such person. Having asked myself those questions—who am I? what am I?—there were aspects to my response that I felt in my deepest recesses were not an expression of *me*, of who I truly am. I chose to utter these aspects when speaking of who I am, but I sensed—or rather, I knew—they were not who I am. They were intruders, invaders, infiltrators, infections; they were *impositions*, compelled upon me as ways to define myself. Or perhaps to put it better, it was as though I had chosen the responses, but the options from which I'd been required to choose were determined for me by someone or something else. I was picking the words, but the dictionary from whence the vocabulary was made available was not from me, and neither was it *for* me. By what seemed a completely unconscious compulsion, I was attempting to describe my identity based on options and boundaries dictated to me by something other than myself; something that did not know me and, indeed, did not care for me.

Thus coming to recognize this predicament, how could I adjust, tweak, or fix my response to describe myself adequately or fully within such a framework? No matter how long I thought or tried, I could not, and hence the result—

Dissatisfaction. Incompletion. Frustration. Unrest.

I would imagine there are a myriad of ways in which the above can manifest itself, and countless variations of how others, including you, might relate. My own journey to the realization and resolution of this problem, however, was shaped primarily by a simple question people would often ask me.

Chapter 2
"Where Are You From?"

"Where are you from?"

On the surface, this question might appear to be of the utmost banality and everyday ordinariness. But what typically prompts it? As someone who has been asked this question his whole life—and likely will continue to be asked until his last days—the answer is rather clear. In a word, it is *difference*.

The question is born from a set of expectations and built-in assumptions tying together a given location, with certain characteristics embodied thereby. Such characteristics might include first-glance appearances like skin tone, hair color, bodily proportions, and facial features, as well as language and accent, general behavior, mannerisms, and "vibe." It is difficult to place a finger on what exactly makes somebody appear to be "from here" as opposed to "from there" or elsewhere, but somehow, it seems we all just know; that is, we all possess in some form or another a deep-seated, almost instinctive understanding, or rather presupposition, that someone from *here* is like *this*, and someone from *there* is like *that*. And upon encountering another, it is an assessment of them through the prism of such a presupposition that triggers the question to be asked.

To be sure, considering that the trigger is the perception of difference, the question is specially reserved for those considered foreign in some sense within the context of the given location, as opposed to the locals and natives who are, for want of a better word, "supposed" to be where they are, and thus are absolved of the scrutiny.

In the case of myself, from as early as I can remember, I understood the primary impetus for being asked this question was the way I looked. It didn't take much in-depth reflection or analysis to figure out that this was the case, for the statement, "ah, you look a bit different," or something along those lines, almost invariably preceded or followed the inquiry to my origins.

For some context, I was born and mostly raised in London, UK, by a British (English and Scottish) father and a Japanese mother. Now, according to common logic, that makes me half British and half Japanese, but *from* a big city called London in a relatively small, cold, rain-and-wind-swept island country called the United Kingdom of Great Britain and Northern Ireland. But it was always puzzling to me that "London" or "Britain" never quite seemed to suffice as an answer to "where are you from?" There seemed to be an unspoken image and assumption of what someone from London or the UK was "supposed" to look like, and somehow I didn't fit this bill.

How I looked—and therefore where I was perceived to be from—was always in the eye of the beholder. Over the years I have encountered a plethora of various speculations and judgments on the possible answer, from Chinese as a young child and teenager to anything from Russian, Italian, Spanish, Kazakh, Afghan, Turkish, or even Native American as an adult. I would often think of myself as a sort of mirror of people's presumptions and perceptions on countries, race, and their relation to appearance—if they thought someone from a given part of the world was supposed to look a certain way, and in one way or another I fit their image as such, that would be their guess on my origins. And curiously, very seldom was it raised as a possibility that I might be British or Japanese and even less often that I could be a mix of the two. The vast majority of people thought very much in terms of singularity, that each person was from *here* or *there*, was *this* or *that*, in accordance with the way this world is organized by countries as singular entities, assumed to be inhabited and "owned" by a single dominant race or nationality. Indeed, as I began to understand this trend I always felt a certain pressure to provide a neat and concise answer, preferably in one word, in conformity with the "standard" comprehension of the world as such; though, as mentioned, this never quite worked out well, since the "correct" answer seemed never to be acceptable and only raised further questions.

For the most part, I suppose the questions and speculations were born from a harmless curiosity about how I looked, which was "a bit different" vis-à-vis people's image and stereotypes. But my appearance also seemed to draw out the more underlying psycho-emotional impulses of people. It was clear that some guesses that I was this or that, from here or there, were driven by a desire to highlight separation—to discriminate, disparage, and assert a person's sense of racial or national superiority, while others seemed to seek fellowship and connection in the hope that

I was in some way the same as them. Like the time when, after a game of 7-a-side soccer, a Somali gentleman came running up to me asking excitedly whether I was Afghan, only to be visibly disappointed when I had to break it to him that I was not (though why he, being Somali, so hoped I was Afghan I do not know). I've witnessed similar disappointment descend upon the faces of the many Turks at kebab shops across the globe who have enquired if I was Turkish, or Russians in London, New York, and Tokyo who were convinced that I was also one of their kind.

Turning the spotlight to myself, it was interesting to observe my own unconscious prejudices on racial hierarchy among the variety of races and nationalities that were put forward to me. It somehow seemed more complementary to be thought of as Italian, Spanish, or Portuguese than Algerian or Kazakh, while Chinese or Mongolian would almost always come across as derogatory and insulting, though this was perhaps because these terms were often meant as a slur. Indeed, while I have encountered countless endearing moments with people playfully guessing my place of origin, it was especially during my years in school that I experienced some quite outrageous racial abuse by those who perceived me as "Chinese" or, as many of them simply put it, a "chinky."

I recall one occasion during the SARS outbreak in 2003, when I was in my early teens, when a light cough from me in a corridor provoked a girl nearby to screw up her face, clamp her hand over her mouth, and mutter "SARS" before walking away in disgust. Or another instance during the same period when, on the walk home from school, a group of girls appeared out of nowhere, laughing like a pack of hyenas, and proceeded to throw a slew of Chinese-sounding names at me whilst mockingly slanting their eyes.

Even in later years as I hit puberty and supposedly became less "Chinese" in my appearance, the racial insults and bullying continued through many who perceived an East-Asian otherness in me. In my penultimate year of secondary school, during a history lesson on the Vietnam War, a classmate pointed to the famous image of General Nguyễn Ngọc Loan executing Nguyễn Văn Lém and blurted out, "Miss, why is Richard in the textbook?" The teacher, I recall, simply gave a lightly despondent look to the culprit pupil before moving onto the next part of the lesson.

And on my first day of induction at high school, in what happened to be one of the best schools in the region, a teacher looked at my profile form, read my mother's name, and asked, seemingly in all seriousness, whether it was "one of those kung fu names." The question was even accompanied by a karate chop and "hi-yah!" sound effects! While I ended up having what were probably the best years of my school life there despite this peculiar start, I nonetheless encountered similar unfortunate moments. Once as I walked down a corridor and passed a group of my peers, a fellow student in a religious studies class turned to his friends and asked with a smirk, "Anyone want to get a Chinese?"

Looking back, it is interesting to observe that these and countless other offenses were perpetrated by people from all sorts of races and ethnic backgrounds. The first two instances above both involved Black girls. The question during the history lesson was asked by a Pakistani Muslim boy, while the teacher was a Muslim woman who donned a chador and, rather ironically, was vehement in her criticism of what she characterized as the anti-Muslim, imperialist crusades of the Afghan and Iraq Wars of 2001 and 2003 respectively. The karate-chopping, kung-fu-sound-effect-making teacher was, I think, of South Indian descent, while the snarky student in the corridor was White.

Now, the point in offering these examples and noting the racial profile of those involved is not simply to tell tales and implicate; rather, it suggests that people of all races and colors are capable of being discriminatory and picking out perceived differences in others for derision—something that I have also been culpable of. And while those involved, if challenged, would surely have dismissed their comments as jokes, the psychological effect it had on me as an impressionable and sensitive adolescent was profound. I was born and lived in one of the most multicultural and supposedly tolerant cities on earth, but I was faced with bullying and abuse that told me unequivocally that I did not belong. The only feelings were of shame; that I was somehow guilty, dirty, and unwanted—rejected and alone, simply because of the way I looked.

Thankfully, as I grew older I managed to forgive and overcome these traumatic instances (I suppose they were intended as jokes after all), and though the chink-bashing would gradually subside as I moved into new environments, the question "where are you from?" never seemed far from the next person's lips. Admittedly, it was rather amusing sometimes to hear the novel, and at times baffling, guesses. And though it wasn't racially inspired bullying akin to the examples of my school years, there was invariably an accompanying sense of unease, anxiety, and embarrassment each time I was posed the question or faced with an obnoxious blurting-out of what someone thought I was without even asking. It was a feeling that was apparent even as a young child, but perhaps due to it being unable to be rationalized by a preadolescent mind, and then ignored as a teenager and young adult as it became an everyday occurrence, it was not until my late twenties that I consciously recognized this feeling and sought on one fateful afternoon to understand my reaction as such.

Maybe there was no reason for a mere question on origins to trouble me, I thought to myself. Indeed, I even had friends who enjoyed sharing their background with anyone who happened to ask. Why couldn't I be more like them? But I understood that "where are you from" was more than just a question. It was also a statement—a declaration—that said *"you are not from here,"* and each time I heard it, I was confronted with my innate foreignness. Certainly, I knew being foreign wasn't bad in and of itself. However, according to my self-analysis, the sense of unease was born and compounded by my desire, or perhaps expectation, to be recognized and associated with what I considered my home countries of Great Britain and Japan, the two places where, if nowhere else, I thought I should be able to say, but more importantly *feel*, that I was from and belonged.

But, alas, it seemed to me that neither place perceived me to be from there. Japan is to this day one of the most ethnically and socially homogenous countries on earth, with the sense of what it means to be Japanese deeply intertwined with all aspects of a person's being—language, behavior, mannerisms, considerations, customs, and appearance—and having lived there as an adult for several years, it was abundantly clear that I was not Japanese according to the common criteria, insofar that the way I looked was in such clear contradiction with the nationally-held self-portrait.

Britain, on the other hand, is a more curious case. Like other Western countries, it attempts to project a more inclusive, nonracial, and predominantly political definition of what it means to be British. The reality is debatable, to say the least, and my experiences of racist abuse from a good number of its inhabitants suggested I should forego the idea that I might be British and "from London," despite common sense and the plain fact that I was.

Indeed, it was curious to observe that a "British" person who—to put it bluntly—wasn't White, was so only with qualification. Such a person would be designated "British-Asian" (which by and large meant Indian, Pakistani or Bangladeshi), "British-Caribbean," "British-Chinese," and so on, while being just "British" seemed only to apply to anyone who could be interpreted as Caucasian, whether they were of English, Scottish, Welsh, Irish, or even Polish or Greek descent, to list a few possibilities within the spectrum of what constituted White. The same seems to be the case across the pond in the USA, where conspicuous minorities are labeled "African-American," "Latino-American," "Asian-American," and so forth, while again the default "American" is the reserve of a person of White ethnicity.[1]

Is Britishness, American-ness, or any other "-ness" of a culturally Western country, inherently tied to Whiteness? I was always somewhat puzzled, for instance, about why Barack Obama quickly became known as the first African-American President, even though his mother was as White as any other "regular" American. Indeed, all Americans—Black, White, Brown, Yellow, Red, and everything in between—seemed united in their designation of him as their first Black President, fully disregarding his mother's ethnicity in determining his racial classification.

One of my own experiences aptly captured this same phenomenon. One day in school when I was fourteen or fifteen

---

[1] This trend was dramatized in hilarious fashion by the viral YouTube video, "What kind of Asian are you?"

years old, one of my mixed-race (half Black and half White) friends referred to himself in conversation as Black. By this time, I had a budding sense of the tension within myself in being half White-British and half Japanese, not knowing to which I belonged and identified with. Hoping perhaps to identify a fellow tortured mongrel soul, I impulsively commented that his mum was White—to which he curtly replied, "So? I'm still Black."

But perhaps the case of Barack Obama, due to its prominence on the world stage, shows us more than any other that the identification of race is more social and political than it is biological. Obama, and it seems all children of mixed African heritage, can self-identify as Black and be accepted by their respective Black communities as one of their own despite the presence of non-Black parentage. Meanwhile, White people typically assume that the child of a White person and someone of another ethnicity is of the other, non-White half of their ethnic make-up or something else entirely. Indeed, the response is similar in Japan, whereby a person of mixed heritage between a Japanese person and another is simply assigned the rather lazy colloquialism of *haafu* (meaning "half"), highlighting their departure from racial purity.

For reasons that are hazy and wide-ranging (a discussion of which is beyond the scope of this work), we have what seems then to be a high degree of Black racial inclusiveness and a White and Japanese racial exclusiveness at the opposite end of the scale. And I was caught in the middle of the exclusivity of the latter two, distanced by both in being consistently asked—or told—"where are you from?" even within the two countries of my heritage. It felt to me as a tacit refutation of the idea that I was *from* either place. You are not from *here*, they seemed to say, because you are not like *this*.

Furthermore, I came to realize that my discomfort with the question lay in the simple fact that I couldn't actually answer it, at least not in the way that people seemed to expect, with a straightforward, one-word nationality or ethnicity. What exactly was the question asking anyway? Where was I born? Where I resided? What country did I associate most with? Or perhaps where people like me were "supposed" to come from (which, as my life experience had shown, could be anywhere). Indeed, being a product of two nationalities meant that I felt I belonged to both—or at least, that I *should* belong to both. But it always seemed to be the assumption of the peoples of those respective countries that I was not, that I belonged somewhere—anywhere—else but *here*.

It was at this point that I felt I came to grips with the principle behind group relationship dynamics. It is a two-way street. You belong to a given group by identifying with the group but also, and perhaps more importantly, by the group identifying with you. As ardently as you may wish or even insist upon being a part of a group, if the group in question does not reciprocate your desire, then you are not a part of the group. You can speak the language, have the accent, wear the clothes, eat the food, think the thoughts, and behave appropriately, but if for whatever reason the group rejects the validity of your membership, then you're not a part of the club. Certainly, one's perception of "the group" is molded inexorably by one's environment and the people encountered therein. Yet in my case, it seemed that wherever I carried myself, the question (where are you from?) was never far away; and the implied statement (you are not from here) was always front of mind.

Thus I was faced with the conundrum: *who* was I, *what* was I, and where was I actually from? And in addition to all that, where would accept me as being "from here"?

The million-dollar question: Where did I belong?

Was I from Britain or Japan? Choosing just one wouldn't work, because that would mean denying the side I did not choose.

Maybe, then, I was from Britain and Japan? This seemed to make sense, and I even had the paperwork to prove it. But based on my experience, neither country saw me as one of their own.

Or rather, was I a half-British and half-Japanese person who, being born and raised in London, was therefore from London? Now this was more like it, closer to a real description of my existence. But the cold reality was being of mixed race meant I looked different, and group relationship dynamics meant I didn't seem to qualify as being from London, or at least I lacked the confidence to tell myself and others that I was.

So maybe I was from London, identified most with Britain, but simultaneously had heritage and influence from Japan? Or maybe... You get the picture.

On and on it went, leading me round in circles and digging deeper into the same hole, with answers and a resolution seemingly none the closer. This wasn't simply a case of a circle not fitting into a square, or vice versa; at least a circle could fit in among other circles and a square among its own. I was a triangle (or whatever), unable to fit in as neither a circle nor a square. A common response to my quandary was, "You're overthinking this way too much. Just say whatever you feel most comfortable with! Nobody cares how you respond anyway." But that was precisely the point—nothing *felt* right. And I wasn't merely trying to describe and justify my existence to another; I was in genuine search of identity and a place to belong. But quite literally nothing fit, and to my despair, it appeared the only choice I had was to vest upon myself a definition, whatever it may be, that was not *me* and to kill those feelings that urged me to keep searching for answers—

Dissatisfaction. Incompletion. Frustration. Unrest.

In very real terms, to kill *me*.

To kill the *truth*.

What truth?

That as a person of mixed race and multinational, multicultural heritage, I am neither one nationality nor another, and not simply half this or half that. I am both, and therefore I am neither. Multiplicity is my identity. For this reason, answering the question "where are you from?" in accordance with the way the world is organized and commonly understood in terms of categorization by a single country, nationality, ethnicity, or any given combination of them, was innately problematic for me. Respecting the truth of my identity—multiplicity—meant I simply could not answer it in any satisfactory way. To identify and define myself in singularity or any combination of singularities, felt tantamount to manifesting the segregation and division of the world within myself. In effect, it would be a segregation and division of self.

Indeed, were not all these concepts known as "countries" simply and precisely that—concepts? In this regard, were they not all just inventions brought about as a means to organize the planet into manageable, measurable blocks, presented to the rest of us as the available options with which to identify? If this was so, why was I for so long attempting to pigeonhole myself into this framework of ideas? That everyone around me—literally, the whole world—felt compelled to do so did not matter. Why did I have to do the same? What obligation was I under to categorize myself within the boundaries set upon me by this world, to define myself only from options provided?

> Options that were—evidently—not for me.
> Options that did not know me, and did not care for me.

Upon asking the question, it was clear—there was no such obligation. There was no outright coercion. There was only my own choice to define myself by these terms, to limit myself to what I *thought* were the only options.

There I sat, alone in my apartment, and in a moment of clarity, I lifted my head from the clutches of my hands as if to liberate myself from all the internal wrangling and turmoil up to this point.

Now it seemed so obvious.

How could the words, categories, and definitions—countries—that I had been choosing from satisfy me if they were not created in my name, and if they were simply dictated to me from above by this world—by *them*? By attempting to define myself only by terms imposed upon me, how could I find *me*?

Sensing that I was now tiptoeing into uncharted, and somehow forbidden territory, I instinctively made a few quick turns of the head to check no one was watching. It was at that moment that I made a dash for it, and in no uncertain terms, simply said out loud:

"*Fuck it.*"

Then I said it again. "*Fuck it all.*"

And at once, I was free.

I was both, I was neither—I was *me*.

Chapter 3
Self Revolution

Within myself, there had been a revolution.

I had made a choice. I had chosen to reject the labels and definitions handed to me as the available options and the sole means to express my identity. I accepted no more the mindset that assumed I needed to be this or that—to agonize over *what* I was—and it was thereby I resisted the control that was being attempted over me. For as long as I chose to abide only by terms imposed upon me, it was the world that defined me and caused me to identify by *what*, rather than *who*, I am. But uttering those two (or three) most defiant and liberating of words (no need to repeat them, however!), for the first time in my life, I had chosen to be *me*.

And I could feel it. At an instant, those all too familiar feelings of discontent had evaporated, transforming instead to pride, joy, and freedom—to power.

I had realized the power within myself—the power to choose, to be *me*, to define myself by my own terms upon the truth of *who I am*.

I am not (country). I am not (nationality). I am not (ethnicity). I am not (whatever).

I am, simply, who I am.
I am *me*.
I am *I*.
I am.

This choice—this revolution—seemed to open up within me an entirely new and different dimension of perspective. No longer bound by constraints and awake to the power *within*, I was free to explore, to discover, to choose.

I had the power, the freedom, to define myself.

Thus began a new chapter of searching, one based not on submission to predetermined options, but strength, freedom, and most importantly, truth—based on *self*. And first on my agenda of questions was, of course, countries.

What were countries anyway? Were they not just arbitrary forms of identification and organization? Indeed, for people like myself, countries did not satisfy as a means to identification, especially given that countries, as we recognize them today, did not always exist but were created as concepts at specific points in time by people like you and me. With thoughts such as these circling in my head, I began to deduce and decipher this seemingly ominous and oppressive concept known as "country" that had so aggrieved me.

Certainly, there are varying interpretations of the origins of countries. A patriot or a romanticist may understand them as manifestations of group identity, either the natural or hard-won products of shared aspirations for autonomy within a given territory. A skeptic or critic, on the other hand, may claim some countries to be merely the stamp of ownership of a certain people over an area of land, often taken and absorbed by force, while others with a similarly critical view might observe that many countries are derived simply from a carving of a map drawn by the pen of an imperialist. Simple and sweeping descriptions perhaps, but ideas pertaining to the origins of today's numerous countries can in most cases be found somewhere within this spectrum.

Realizing that the more critical or pessimistic views seemed to treat countries as invalid by definition, I felt I ought to unwrap further the view that was in many respects the least comfortable. That is, that countries serve as representations of the inhabiting people, as an embodiment and collection of ideals that, especially in times of danger and strife, serve as a source of strength and solidarity, a point of unity in the name of a higher cause. In this view, I was forced to consider that the concept of countries might be a good thing. Perhaps it was simply that my grievances were misplaced all along and I needed to rethink my entire position?

To my surprise, I concluded that there was much about this understanding of countries to embrace, but for one important exception. This concept more accurately described a *nation*, that is, a coming-together of a given number of people upon similar cultural foundations and aspirations. A nation in this regard is an entirely organic, ground-up entity, in contrast to the *state*, which consists of apparatus and institutions created to rule, govern, and control a nation and its people. A country, then, is best understood as the name or label describing the entity known as a "nation-state," in which the people and ruling bodies within defined borders are conflated into one.

Based on this analysis, I knew my beef lay not with nations and the everyday people around me, but with states and—yes—countries. For in my mind, that countries were merely labels was an immovable fact. Delving further, it was clear they were also a form of *imposition*, terms by which people designated as "from here" or "from there" were made to identify and define themselves, with all the associated assumptions of how people "should be" thereupon. In this regard, countries are also synonymous with categorization, that is, imposition *through* categorization, and the mindsets of the peoples of nations were molded inextricably according to the lines of division that countries created. And further still, it was apparent that the existence of countries as a top-down, artificial labeling of a given geographical area was underpinned by the *system* of segregated and sovereign states,[2] a system which imposed borders upon nations as a means to determine the jurisdiction of states and governments, and to compartmentalize sections of this planet into separate and competing entities.

For me it was clear that states viewed and treated nations as a mere resource. They were a reservoir of human resource, from which they drew soldiers for armies and workers for economies, and from whom they collected taxes to fund their exploits. Essentially, peoples of nations were servants of the state, and the latter

---

[2] This is referring to the concept of state sovereignty that emerged from the Peace of Westphalia in 1648, which forms the basis of the modern international state system.

conducted all manner of surveillance, deception, and propaganda to keep the former in position as such, nullifying and eliminating any threats that might emanate from among the people who have ideas otherwise. And it was within the system and arena of global affairs that states competed with others, vying for position and advantage, cooperating solely out of self-interest and necessity. Indeed, the system ascribes the label of *country* to describe the nation-state as one body (or rather, two bodies made into one), under the notion that states represent nations and that nations *belong* to states. The system thereby compounds this relationship of rulers and subjects (that is, governments and citizens), reinforcing the assumption that nations and states are one and the same, that the state is part of the nation, when the reality seems to suggest the relationship is far from one of equals with mutual respect and benefits.

Ah, but that is why we have a democracy, you might say, but more on that later. The burning question on my mind at the time was why we go along with the status quo of the system as such and choose to live within its assumptions and boundaries. For it seemed states sought nothing but servitude and obedience from nations, and the system created only lines of segregation, division, and competition between countries. We so often hear that "countries go to war," but how often do nations, that is, the people themselves, have a death wish against another? It is the people who fight the wars, but is it ever *the people's* war? Or rather, are wars, with few exceptions, invariably caused by states for the sake of states, with the peoples of nations hoodwinked, bamboozled, and led astray to fight the wars on their behalf?

Since the lawful exercise of violence has become the sole reserve of states, one has to squint very hard to find examples of wars waged solely, or even predominantly, to safeguard the security of the people of nations, as opposed to promoting state power and the interests of elites, for whom the state operates and exists. Certainly, conflicts are always packaged and propagandized as the former (for "the greater good"), to convince the common people who make up the ranks of soldiers and the wider public who must bear the burden for any given war effort. But to ask again—is it ever the people's war? Or is it simply the war of those who would command us to fight?

This was a question that I was personally able to ponder and confront, partly owing to a single year that I spent enlisted in the British Army Reserve. My interest in the military began with some relevant family history, but was mostly born from a simple boyish enthusiasm for rugged adventure and just how cool soldiers seemed to look in camouflage, flak jackets, and helmet-mounted headsets. And though I did seriously consider joining the Regular Army as a career path, it was through a debacle during the selection process that I ultimately concluded that I was "too Japanese" to join the British armed forces on a full-time basis and landed in the Army Reserve instead.[3]

But even from what was a very short-lived stint riddled with struggle, in which I admittedly spent more time feeling inadequate and miserable about myself rather than reflecting on the wider intellectual implications of my predicament, I managed to somehow draw out just enough to sketch out a position on the malevolence of states and the futility of war in their name. This is not to say that one does not attain valuable, even life-changing

---

[3] This is not to suggest that I personally suffered racial discrimination or abuse whilst attempting to join the Regular Army; it was simply my perception of my own suitability for what is *the* quintessential British institution alongside the monarchy.

rewards from time spent in the military. Even I was able to glean invaluable lessons, and one instance in particular had a profound effect.

It was during one of the introductory sessions on handling a rifle, taking place in an empty classroom with no tables or chairs, just bare walls, a moveable whiteboard, and a floor carpeted with material too thin to soften the concrete below. My section was being instructed on the various shooting positions—standing, kneeling, sitting, and prone. It was whilst in this latter position—laying down on one's belly, with the right leg bent so that the inside of the knee is flat against the floor and the elbows supporting the rifle from the ground—that our group faced particular difficulty, with the hard floor causing severe pain and discomfort, especially on the bent knee and elbows. Our corporal, seeing us squirming and fidgeting in distress whilst he tried to explain the fundamentals of the position, interrupted his lecture and stood us to attention. After a few choice words to express his dissatisfaction with our lack of durability, he paused, his demeanor changed, and he said to us in a noticeably more compassionate tone, "All situations, no matter how difficult, always end. So just grit your teeth, and fucking *get through it.*"

The wording perhaps was not the most eloquent or philosophical, and the setting of the speech even less so. But it was in this moment that, for the first time in my life, I felt I consciously grasped what it means to persevere, to keep moving forward in spite of pain or trouble, with the hope and knowledge that the suffering will end. I wasn't the hardiest of men when I joined the Army Reserve, and most certainly I still am not; but after this unexpected lesson in the most unspectacular of circumstances, I left that classroom with a lump in my throat and eyes tearing up—

the impact of the lesson clearly getting to me—perhaps just a little bit tougher than when I had entered. Indeed, the advice from our corporal that day has stood me in good stead during hard times ever since.

But perhaps my greatest learning experience, if I can call it that, related to the Army Reserve came not during any particular exercise or activity, but rather from a dream I had a few years after I had been voluntarily discharged.

The setting was somewhere in England. In the midst of typical English weather (wet and windy), my squad was taking part in a training exercise that required us to pull heavy backpacks and large fuel canisters from the back of a truck and carry them up a hill. As was the case throughout my time in the Army, even during my dream I struggled with my confidence and to generally get involved, and every time I laid eyes on a free item, it seemed to immediately get taken by somebody else. Whilst generally buzzing about, trying to look like I was contributing but not actually doing much, a few big backpacks and canisters fell from the truck to the ground before me, and again they were immediately surrounded and picked up by other squad members, two of whom were already seemingly at their limit in terms of the load they were carrying. One of them attempted to take up yet another one of these backpacks, and his comrade next to him, also carrying more than his fair share, encouraged and helped him to do so. As I witnessed this, my only thought was to somehow get involved and alleviate the guilt I was feeling from not being able to do so. Pointing out that I had nothing on my hands yet, I pulled the backpack off this person, saying it was too heavy. Upon my intervention, the two got very annoyed and asked what I was doing, then pulled the backpack onto themselves again, turned, and marched up the hill.

The setting in my dream then changes to what I think was the aftermath of the exercise, where a nameless female corporal takes me to a shack with various military gear and machinery lying around. Calling me by my first name, the corporal mentions she is very disappointed in me for that attempt at the exercise and with my presence in the Army generally. She then picks off a piece of metal from a machine next to her and bites into it in an attempt to create a shape of some sort. I wince at seeing this, and as with the squad members during the exercise, I attempt to stop her, thinking it was painful and unnecessary. But she succeeds in whatever she was trying to accomplish and simply throws away the piece of metal before I could intervene. At this point, the conversation turns more casual, and she says to me, "We need more good-looking soldiers like you." Perhaps due to the embarrassment from having been complimented (about my looks no less) but also the sense of having let her and myself down with a poor showing at the exercise, I awoke and was back in my bed.

To this day, I am not entirely certain of the implication or meaning (if there is any at all) behind the metal-biting corporal. I did find it curious that I was complimented on the way I looked, for although the last instance of overt racist bullying I experienced was some years ago by this time, it was still my perception that I looked and was different from those around me, which bred a sense of inferiority and a lack of confidence that I carried throughout my time in the Army. But other than this interpretation which wasn't exactly news to me, I haven't managed to fathom any particular learning or insightful reflection. Quite the opposite was the case, however, with the exercise with the squad members, the lesson of which was clear to me from the moment I opened my eyes.

Faced with the men hauling loads seemingly beyond their capacity, my primary mistake lay in attempting to stop them from what I perceived were actions they could not, or rather should not, try to carry out. Along with my own inability to get involved, I had simply made myself doubly unhelpful by interfering with men who were demonstrating that they were willing and able to do more. Witnessing their selflessness and determination, my reaction should have been simply to trust, to recognize that they were capable, to help the loading on rather than interfering with it, and to look them in the eyes and offer words of encouragement before letting them "crack on" (Army-speak meaning "carry on" or "go ahead"). To behave in such a way—to act as a hand helping to push the limits of those around you, to assist in the breaking of boundaries rather than placing limitations or restrictions—would have been in the true spirit of Army leadership and comradery.

Upon awakening to this realization, I was overwhelmed by a sense of regret. Though it was just a dream, and I cannot recall an actual instance when I behaved in this manner whilst in the Army Reserve, I nonetheless felt it reflected a certain tendency within me, born from a damaged confidence and a subsequent inability to act assuredly. It felt as if the dream had actually happened, and I fully shared in the sense of disappointment expressed by the nameless corporal towards myself. Since this dream occurred long after I had been discharged, perhaps it is a shame that I didn't experience a similar situation while I was in the Army, and did not have the chance earlier to overcome what was an actual weakness of mine. But as with all learning and growth in life, I had to take it as a case of better late than never, better through a dream than not at all. Needless to say, I have taken the lessons of this dream to heart and I am grateful for the greater self-awareness it has provided me, as well as a perspective on leadership that I did not possess previously.

In this regard, I know from my own experience the positive benefits that military service and training can provide to an individual, even if it is as limited and short-lived as my own. Indeed, some of the recruits and staff I had the privilege of spending time with were, in the most unobtrusive of ways, truly remarkable people with steadfast dedication, loyalty, kindness, and humor to match their tough doggedness; and I am sure the Army and wider military is littered with such men and women throughout.

With my personal military experience and the people who make up its ranks, then, I have no qualms. What did bother me, both as a recruit and now, was the ultimate end to which we were made to train and work—that is, through lethal means or otherwise, to neutralize whoever and whatever is deemed an enemy by the state.

While the Army and wider military foster an admirable culture of discipline, teamwork, and self-sacrifice, as well as an emphasis on personal excellence and valor, all these qualities and indeed the organization of the military itself are directed and purposed above all for the advancement of state aims, which to me seemed anything but patriotic or "for the good of the people." Though respective military leaders may inspire their troops to push limits and boundaries, they, or rather the state they serve, saddles each individual with a them-against-us mentality, which is both inherently limiting and a prerequisite for belligerency and conflict.

And it is important to note that this manipulation of perception—a sort of brainwashing—is a feature of all states, countries, and even non-state actors that have not eschewed violence, with one labeling another as an enemy. In all camps there is the attempt to dehumanize the opposition so that each person belonging to the opposing camp is seen merely as a conflation and extension of the enemy state, government, country, group, or whatever entity is labeled a threat; and this to the end of snuffing out a view of "the other" as fellow human beings, with fears, hopes, dreams, pressures, worries, opinions, convictions, traumas, and scars— just like us all.

When we are marched into battle, do we know our so-called enemies?

Do we even attempt to empathize and seek to understand the person we confront?

And if we did, would we still see them as *our* enemies?
Would it still be *our* war?

Or would we see through the smokescreens that blind us and recognize that we who fight are the same as those we fight against, that for both us and our so-called enemies, the same set of hands are pulling the strings?

For when war in our current age is understood to primarily be an instrument of policy, simply a means for states to consolidate and expand power through the exercise of violence, then the illusion that "we are all in this together," that it is *our* war, withers and fades. But such is the tragedy and indeed the crime behind every such conflict, that military personnel are put in circumstances of tremendous danger, stress, and pressure to fight a war that is not their doing nor in their best interests. Indeed, war and conflict as state policy is a most sinister form of blackmail, in which soldiers are commanded by their military and political leaders to fight on behalf of the state and elites, lest they be harmed or killed in the line of fire—"Kill the enemy," they are ordered, "or you and your friends will die." What a terrifying predicament to be placed in, and yet the state and elites are so willing, so enthusiastic, so happy to place these men and women on the battlefield. Certainly, most members of the armed forces deal with their situation with the most incredible bravery and selfless commitment—indeed, many are irreversibly injured or even die to protect their friends fighting alongside them—traits that are in total contrast to those of the "leaders" who send them to fight.

They are utterly selfless; their leaders are utterly selfish.

They are the epitome of courage; their leaders the definition of cowardice, spineless manipulators who would send others to fight *their* war, using the lie of a common good as justification.

And yet, it is the soldiers who suffer trauma, while their leaders sleep comfortably.

It is the soldiers who die, and their leaders—the instigators—who live.

How much longer before we wake up to this injustice—this deception—that is war?

How many more wars will it take before we finally refuse to fight for the narrow self-interests of states and their mere handful of beneficiaries?

Alas, war will not cease while the peoples of nations continue to be deceived to fight and generally act on the state's behalf, especially for aims that are achieved at the expense of other nations. To this end, states partaking in this system of countries will create and exacerbate the artificial fault lines that divide people. How and why would we fight, kill, and imprison the people of another nation unless we believed in the idea—the lie—that they were a type of *other* and, further, that we from *this* country are superior and somehow better than people from *that* country?

When will we wake up to our fundamental unity and disengage our crosshairs from so-called enemies, who have been led astray by their manipulators and labeled a threat, just as we ourselves have?

When will we see that the adversary is not across from us, on the other side of the battlefield, but rather above us, in the form of the "leaders" and state machinery that command us to kill on their behalf?

When will we awaken to the truth that you and I are the same, that there is no better or worse, high or low, superior or inferior?

That I am simply *I*, and you are simply *you*?

For it is thus that we shed our imposed labels, and cease to be separated by borders. It is by this realization that we rid ourselves of the lines that divide and the boundaries that separate.

Thus there will no longer be limits—no sides and therefore no enemies.

Only unity—a band—between you and me.

Chapter 4
Self Resolution

Although states and the system in which they operate seem only to foster separation and peoples of nations have become poisoned by such a mindset, throughout my still-short life I have been struck by the ability, or rather what seems to be an innate tendency, of people to find commonality and form bonds of connection with one another. Though on many days, the forces of rejection, disparagement, and division have seemed much more apparent in my own life and the world at large (all it takes is a short glance at the news, if ever I needed reminding), concurrent with the enmity there is still an abundance of fellowship and harmony. Certainly, it may take a bit of effort to reflect and notice the goodness around us, especially if we are in oppressive and hostile circumstances. But I for one was fortunate in that everywhere and every day I could discern acts of altruism, empathy, charity, and solidarity all around me, seemingly enacted regardless of country and questions of origin, done simply out of the unconditional goodness and humanity of people.

Further, I was surrounded by so much that radiated color, variety, flavor, and life in the form of culture. And of all the manifestations of culture, it was most particularly in music, especially in a live setting, that I've sensed and experienced tremendous power to create commonality and a cause to transcend differences among people within a country's borders and those between nations.

If you've ever been to a live gig, I suspect you know exactly what I'm talking about. When a group of people gather through a common love of the sound, there is a special sense of unity—centered on the artist but also with each individual present—that can be felt with every fiber of one's being. For the duration of the song and the set, nothing else matters but the music and the sheer enjoyment of it, and all who are present are momentarily one and the same—each is simply who they are, a unique point of attention within a greater body of oneness and totality, bound and redeemed by the unifying power of sound, with no wall or separation to cause division between them. There is no care of where we come from, only that we are *here*. No care of what we are, only that we are the same. No care of who we are, only that we are.

Indeed, the wonder of music goes beyond its ability to bring together disparate individuals into a unified whole. Even in solitude, the capacity for the composing artist to reach out to the listener, to comfort, console, excite, empathize, challenge, confront, charm, and entertain, is felt in the fathomless depths of the soul. The sound conveys energy and emotion from artist to listener, creating an inexplicable bond of companionship and mutual understanding—of friendship—though chances are they have never met and never will. It is a form of communion that transcends time, place, context, and even language, truly a connection of consciousness that attests to our innermost and fundamental oneness.

Through the medium of music, I have come to know of the immense unifying potential of culture, and I am sure all other forms of it, in some way or another, are capable of having a similar effect. However, it is often the case that we conflate culture with countries, seeing the former as the product of the latter. A given culture is perceived to be "owned" by the country from which it happened to originate. In this regard, it is not uncommon for culture to be weaponized by belligerent and unscrupulous minds, laying a claim that "this culture is solely for us" and inhibiting its sharing and partaking for any who might be deemed an "other" in some way. Culture is thus abused as a means to instill a them-against-us—or a "we're-better-than-them"—mentality.

We see this when states seek to hijack and assimilate any new or existing culture within its jurisdiction as belonging to or representing "the country," with the state and corporate vultures exploiting it for political or financial commodification. Among the peoples of nations trapped within the borders of state-imposed countries, many have come to view their cultures in a similar vein, that is, to falsely conflate culture with country, which at its root is born from the fallacy that the two are the same and interchangeable. For indeed, to my mind, culture is always the creation of people and nations; it has nothing to do with countries and the mere labels that they are. The pioneers of any given culture would in this sense be correct in insisting that their culture belongs to them as a people; though again, it is unfortunate that this sentiment often translates into a certain selfishness that disallows sharing and intercourse, and results not in unity but segregation.

Nonetheless, culture was apparent before countries came into existence as we see them today and continues to thrive irrespective of countries (and certainly of the state, government, or corporations). For if we understand any manifestation of culture primarily as a form of *expression*, then it begins to be recognized as something that emanates organically from *within*. Culture is the release, a projection of the world within unto the world without, the cumulative, unified creativity and spirituality of people made tangible. Culture in this respect is also identity, that is, an expression of collective identity. It is a place of belonging.

In addition to its unifying abilities, the power of culture is also apparent in its ability to build bridges, the means by which an individual or a people bestow their expression to another to create connection. Indeed, upon this communion of expression, we often bear witness to a wondrous process of interpretation and re-creation, in which one culture gives influence and inspiration for another, to conjure a new form of expression entirely.

Culture, in a word then, is expression, and it is within culture—collective expression—that we form and find an identity as people. These aspects of culture have no grounding in the concept of countries, the existence of states, and the world system. If anything, culture occurs *despite* the imposing of borders and separation, and indeed, it is the force that serves to overcome separation and to build bridges between people. Though countries, states, and the system conspire to divide peoples of nations in order to pitch them against one another—and tragically, it is often the case that people are susceptible to such corrupting influences—simultaneously, it is the humanity of people themselves and their collective expression as culture that serves to unite them, to fight against that which divides them.

Through this exploration, I began to sense a new way of approaching the question of my identity and where I belonged. Choosing to see *culture* rather than country as a community of belonging, suddenly meant that I belonged not only here, but also there, and in so many other places and environments that expressed a culture that spoke true to me. Whereas countries attempt to force an artificial means of separation and identification based on place, color, race, or ethnicity, culture in its purest, uncorrupted form seeks commonality through a shared resonance of expression and even welcomes difference as diversity, as the source of inspiration for new creation.

For a while at least, this shift in understanding enabled a level of optimism that I had not previously experienced. Indeed, it seemed as though I finally had clear answers to my existential questions: Who am I? I am *me*. What am I? I am multiplicity—of ethnicity, of nationality, of culture. Though the question "where are you from?" was always around the corner, for the first time I had answers that seemed to provide stable ground, and thus the implication of non-belonging no longer caused the embarrassment, confusion, and pain it once did.

But almost as soon as I thought I had arrived at firm conclusions, new depths began to emerge and my inquiry, which up to this point was more or less confined to countries, race, ethnicity, and culture, took on a distinctly spiritual dimension. It was not a development entirely without context, however, for there was a religious framework to my upbringing and I had always nominally claimed to be Christian due to the beliefs of my parents. God, prayer, the spiritual realm, and a rejection of worldly standards of morality were thus conspicuous facets of my life growing up, although, as is difficult to avoid in this age of scientific and rationalist skepticism, my belief in such matters ebbed and flowed with time. I had seen a blissful acceptance in childhood turn into sophomoric rebellion during my late teens and early twenties, interspersed by a number of revivals that quickly died down amidst the drab realities of modern life.

But by the time I was seriously grappling with my identity, I intuitively recognized the existence of God after having overcome a brief flirtation with atheism several years prior. Why, and based on what conception of God was not entirely clear during that earlier period of questioning, but after having consumed various narratives negating God,[4] the supernatural, or anything considered "unscientific" over the course of some years (and even having declared myself an atheist for one brief moment), I found that I simply could not rid myself of the *feeling* that something ineffable—which my cultural vocabulary referred to as "God"—was present, especially in the sense of a creative force or "Mind" that had brought the cosmos into existence.

I understood that the popular disposition of society was to disregard such feelings, that is, to *think* beyond them through appealing solely to intellectual logic and rational argumentation. But how much information would be sufficient to make a "rational" judgment on something as vast and mysterious as God? And even if one arbitrarily determined that enough information had been accumulated (as many of the most prominent atheists of our time

---

[4] Some examples include the works of Antony Flew (who came to accept the existence of a deity later in his life), Richard Dawkins' *The God Delusion* (Black Swan, 2007), *Atheism: A Very Short Introduction* by Julian Baggini (Oxford University Press, 2003), as well as interaction with the objections found in the problems of evil and suffering. A great discussion on these topics was had during a debate I attended between William Lane Craig and Stephen Law in London, October 2011.

have), how warranted would that conviction be when there is so much that is not known? Such misgivings were beside the actual arguments for atheism, which were almost invariably founded on the perceived absence of *scientific* evidence and an unquestioned assumption that the scientific method was the best, or the only, means to figure out a conclusion on God's existence. Considering the broad spectrum of opinion among scientists, mathematicians, philosophers, etc., whether the evidence pointed to God seemed to me a matter of perspective, but I doubted if this was even what science was for.

Better trust my intuition then, I thought, acknowledging the limits of dialectical reasoning and, indeed, the countless times my intuition had been proven right despite the apparent lack of coherent logic. Thenceforward, I happily accepted myself as a believer in a creator God. Considering I had no sense of what role God played apart from creation *ex nihilo*, however, it was a belief that admittedly had very little bearing on my day-to-day life over the next few years. But, as it so happened, God rapidly came to the fore as my questioning around personal identity intensified and would eventually occupy center stage.

Perhaps it was inevitable that it did. If I acknowledged God as the creator and source of all things and that God had created freely and without coercion (something I assumed considering it was God after all), then it followed that all things were extensions and manifestations of the creator. In a sense, creation was the *self-expression* of God. Everything was imbued with meaning and purpose—an *identity*—that was fashioned by the creator and imprinted indelibly onto creation. And through all my struggles with countries, race, and nationality, was it not this essential truth of myself that I was seeking? Naturally, then, the search must lead to

God as the one who had imparted this truth.

It was a simple logic that seemed to be playing out directly as my experience, for it was amply clear that, throughout this whole ordeal, I was not attempting to create an identity for myself but rather was trying to discover *what was already there*. The person that I am transcended the categories and definitions provided by the world, society, and its systems, for my identity had always been within me and could not be molded and conformed to imposed boundaries. It might be that in many respects I was influenced by the world, in terms of the languages I spoke, the way I dressed, the people I knew, the activities I pursued, and even the variety of experiences that shaped my life. But beneath and beyond it all, there was an unchangeable, indivisible, spiritual core and essence—a truth—that was the real *me*.

A truth that could not be defined by the world for it was not from the world.

A truth that was derived from God and bestowed to me as my identity.

A truth—my identity—that I did not choose but had chosen me; one that I needed to encounter, understand, and *become* in order to be *me*.

To this end, I had to resist everything from the world that told me I am to be this or that, based solely on the options that it provided. I also had to relinquish the more insidious idea that it is me who creates my own truth through conscious thoughts and choices. Certainly, I had the power to define myself however I wished, as was my prerogative to resist the labels of countries, for example. But based on what, then, should I define myself? Nothing from the world and not even myself could conjure up an identity of any adequacy or lasting satisfaction—they couldn't grant me truth nor *life* in the truest sense, one that is most authentic, genuine, and expressive of who I truly am. This must be grounded on God alone, for the truth of who I am was derived from God.

I could sense a second revolution burgeoning from my depths. And at the point that these ideas began to take shape, the same declaration echoed in my mind:

I am not (country). I am not (nationality). I am not (ethnicity). I am not (whatever).

I am who I am.
I am *me*.
I am *I*.
I am.

Only this time, I knew it was more than a revolution—it was *resolution*.

Chapter 5
Towards A New World

I had returned to the source of my identity and, indeed, of all things—to God. The ground upon which I now stood was not just firm, it was unshakeable. And it was so not only because I seemed to have found "myself" but, paradoxically, precisely because it was *not* merely myself. Who, and what, I truly am was completely independent of both what the world and I may think I am; it was even independent of any science that informs how our brains operate and the way this influences our thoughts, desires, and personality. For this was not a question of the mechanics of my physical existence, but rather of spiritual truth and identity—an *image* of who I am—that is derived only from God, and however far the frontiers of science may advance, whatever labels the world imposes, or even how I choose to define myself could not change the truth.

Unsurprisingly, these new perspectives had quite an explosive impact as they began to take root in my mind. As exciting as the discoveries were, however, they also caused a significant level of distress as they were such a radical departure from anything I had known previously. Living in a society that was dominated by views of materialism and rationalist skepticism, with increasingly politicized and fraught debates on identity to boot, I was suddenly faced with the idea that, of all things, God was my maker. Further, that God *knew* who I was—who I was supposed to be, according to the truth—and that I was required to align with this ideal to be myself in the truest sense. My understanding of my true self was admittedly still blurred and hazy as if my eyes were only just beginning to open from a deep and prolonged stupor. But as crazy and irrational as it seemed, I felt I was beginning to see.

As the scales fell from my eyes, however, it quickly began to dawn on me that I had been in complete ignorance of who I was up to that point and that my entire life had been constructed under the shadow of this ignorance. Thus, my life no longer appeared to me as a reflection of who I was. Though I had made all the choices to create my circumstances, now it was clear that those choices were made in darkness and a state of blindness. I did not know who I was, hence I had been powerless to make choices as a means to self-expression. As a result, I was inhabiting a world that was not *me* and in which my true self was distant and alienated; a world in which *those* feelings began to make themselves apparent again—

Dissatisfaction. Incompletion. Frustration. Unrest.

A world in which my true self was not alive.
Rather, with each passing day, it was suffocating—dying.

Such realizations burst open that crucial question again—where did I belong? If I was now a stranger even to the circumstances that I had brought upon myself, how could I expect to belong to any that were created by others? Indeed, considering the adoption of these new ideas seemed tantamount to a complete rejection of the world as I found it, was it even reasonable to think anymore that the world could, or even should, provide a place of belonging?

To my mind, the answer was clear: no. The world did not owe me anything and hence it would not provide anything or anywhere. But frankly, by this point, I did not want or need it to. Attempting to find belonging within any pre-existing environment would require conformity to it, that is, I would have to mold the truth of myself to the world rather than vice versa. And with the dissatisfaction and sense of claustrophobia this would inevitably entail, I knew it was a futile endeavor.

It was at that moment a striking idea flashed into my mind: *I had to create my world.* If the world wouldn't cater to my identity (and, to say again, it was not in any way obliged to) then it was up to me to empower myself, take responsibility, and build a world where I would fully belong—a world of my expression and truth.

I felt this to be an incredible thought. Not because of its profundity in any sense, but precisely because it was so simple and obvious. Indeed, there were echoes of my previous breakthrough when I first came to grips with my freedom to define myself, except now it was not merely conceptual but actual—this process of introspection was beginning to have real, practical implications, that is, my self-discovery was quickly evolving into *self-actualization*. Which was unsettling as it was inspiring and exhilarating. Not simply because I had lived to that point following a "standard" path of life, having invested considerable effort in attaining good grades at school, going to college, building a career, etc., but more because I knew it was me who would work to create this new world for myself—not society, the government, the state, or any corporation or institution.

Me.

Who else could? My identity had been bestowed to me and me alone—by definition, therefore, it was impossible for anyone or anything else to do this for me. And that was a rather terrifying thought.

After dwelling on these revelations for some time and pondering their implications, the moment of judgment soon arrived. Despite several attempts to negotiate or find some wriggle room, I was confronted with a simple but most daunting choice: face the truth and live to honor it, or run away.

One side was *me*, the other was somebody else.
One side was truth, the other was untruth—a lie.
One side was life, the other was death.

There was no third way, middle ground, or happy medium. It was one or the other, total and absolute. If I was to live according to the truth of my identity, I would go wherever it takes me and carry out everything it demands to the best of my abilities. I would have to come clean to create this new world of truth and expression—let go of my hitherto lifestyle, walk away from my circumstances, and give up the material trappings I had accumulated. I had to accept that I was no longer going to be in control, that as my identity had been fashioned by God, so too was there a destiny authored by God. It was a frightening paradox, but I had to renounce control and lose myself in order to become myself. This was going to be a journey—a commitment—that would necessarily impact all areas of my existence. The transformation may certainly be gradual, but ultimately there could be nothing that remains unaffected and no stone that stays unturned.

It would be, in the truest sense, rebirth and new life.

And so it was. I made the choice. Though I may not have been giving up a millionaire's champagne lifestyle, bit by bit, I made the sacrifices that I deemed were required of me such as leaving a rewarding career, ending certain relationships, moving out from the city I was living in, and giving up an array of possessions—and it was not by any means easy. But this was the one life I had on this earth and I was determined to live it right, in the way only I could according to the truth of who I was.

One might say it was a rash decision based on the primacy we tend to place on stability, but it was for me an irresistible one as the natural outcome to my searching. In this respect, though it might have been the most outwardly dramatic occurrence thus far, it was also the culmination of a winding inward process preceding it and a bridge to whatever may lie in wait—this was but another step in a journey that had already begun and will long continue. And, if anything, my resolve has only strengthened as I've walked this path. I have found bountiful reserves of trust in God that I had no idea I harbored, and if ever panic or anxiety begins to take hold, I am always reminded of the magically reassuring lyrics to the song *Amazing Grace*—

> *T'was Grace that brought us safe thus far*
> *And Grace will lead us home*

Incidentally, it has been this very book that has served as the platform for my transformation. Though its genesis lies in the crucible of my dissatisfactions, delving into my innermost thoughts and feelings saw this project grow in tandem with myself, becoming the organizing idea by which my true self has finally found a release. And while I owe it to this book for countless new perspectives and micro-evolutions, the greatest gift it has provided has been the development of what can only be described as a profound affinity—namely, faith—in the person of Jesus Christ.

The thoughts that led to my discovery of Jesus will be expounded in a later chapter, but for now, I can only say that it was indeed a peculiar and totally unexpected development. For despite my nominal claims to be Christian and even having had a few fleeting experiences involving Christ, he was completely absent from my consciousness for close to ten years before spontaneously reappearing. Since then, I have often meditated on why he did and why I have so readily embraced all that I have subsequently discovered about him. Was it simply the case that a seed sown into my subconscious earlier in life had coincidentally sprouted and, having left behind society's framework of rationality and predictability, I was now conveniently grasping at comforting mysteries for reassurance?

Perhaps this was partially true, plus that I was already fertile ground having undergone a search for truth and identity in a distinctly spiritual way. But aside from pure faith which, to be sure, is the basis of how and why I believe in Jesus, I have come to the simple conclusion that Jesus came for people like me.

Just as during his ministry he gathered his disciples from among fishermen and tax collectors, proclaiming the coming kingdom of God and pronouncing blessings to the poor and marginalized before anyone, Jesus grants mercy and companionship to outcasts, the disenfranchised, the lowly, and unredeemed who do not find belonging or acceptance. For those of us who are heavy-hearted and weary in a world that does not offer welcome or stay, Jesus extends himself as a place of solace; but more, he invites us to replace all our burdens with his offering—a yoke that is easy, and a burden that is light.[5]

In this way, I believe Christ offers us a deep compassion to support us in our troubles by placing upon ourselves his love. And above all, it is this love that gives me the strange but wonderful sense that, as well as for people *like* me, Jesus came specifically *for* me. This man who was born over two thousand years ago in a distant land somehow lives on to this day to care for me personally; to deal with my struggles and liberate me from my pain. Even without me having fully accomplished my newfound purpose of self-actualization (which will certainly be a lifelong endeavor), in Christ there is always refuge and a home to which I belong. Indeed, it is precisely because of Christ's shelter that I am able to take on this challenge with total confidence and security, knowing that I am loved no matter my shortcomings or the suffering inflicted on me by a broken world.

So it is with the love of Christ and the truth of God inscribed unto my heart, that I venture forward to create a new world—my world.

---

[5] Matthew 11:30

Let it be a world without limitation or confinement, a world of cultural communion and expression of truth.

A world founded on my awareness and knowledge of self; a world that grows as I evolve, but anchored always to my imparted identity—to God.

Let it be a world—a home—where I belong; and if it be possible, a shelter for the searching, a commune for the unbelonging, and a beacon of light for those in darkness.

By the grace of God and the inspiration of Christ, let it be.

Chapter 6
Tips and Takeaways

So that's my story in a nutshell. Though certainly it is "about me," I hope you're able to derive from it some inspiration and food for thought. Maybe you've felt the same way about some of the questions and topics I wrestled with? Or perhaps it allowed you an insight into a point of view you hadn't before encountered. If nothing else, however, I hope it nudges you to be even just a bit more considerate when asking someone *that* question, you know, that seemingly innocuous, four-word question that instigated all of this! But if you would allow me to offer a few tips and takeaways based on my experience, first and foremost, I will say this:

>You are free.
>And you have the power to make choices.

>Just as I am *me*, you are *you*, and there is none but ourselves

who can choose to be this person, who we truly are. Because the power to do so lies within. It is not requisite on any permission or authorization, and indeed, neither is what you discover upon making the choice. Certainly, there might appear to be so much—too much—of this world that attempts to impose upon you an identity and the mental framework within which you think and decide who you are. But to assume an identity within these boundaries, to think and decide based merely on options provided, is again a choice we make. It is up to us to choose whether to base our identity on ourselves or on something that is not—to live as *I* or to live as, and for, *them*. And just because you think you may have already made choices and become *someone*, there is nothing to stop you from making changes to become *you*. Just as you have the power to choose that which you define yourself by, it is also within you to redefine yourself.

So by all means, ask yourself questions. Do not take anything for granted. Do not hold back and assume you are *this* or *that* before you seriously consider whether it actually is who you are. On the same note, we must refuse to settle for anything we know and feel is *not* who we are. That is, we must always heed and follow *those* feelings—

Dissatisfaction. Incompletion. Frustration. Unrest.

These are feelings that call to you, expressing discontent about a situation, an identity, a *life* that is not in accordance with your nature and thus urging you to take a deep, honest look at yourself. Certainly, this takes tremendous courage, because there is risk involved in acknowledging that you are not in fact being *you*. But it is crucial that each of us do so, for without this questioning and honesty, nothing can start—the authentic *you* cannot begin to live.

A second word of advice I would like to offer is to follow your intuition, especially when making judgments on certain ideas. Based on my own experience, it has been proven to me time and again that my intuition possesses oceans of wisdom beyond my conscious reasoning. Even though there is seldom a clear logic to its direction, following its prompts has always led to its vindication.

From my story, this was most obviously demonstrated in relation to my questioning of God's existence and this offers a typical case in point. Having weighed up a good number of arguments for and against, there wasn't any definitive evidence to essentially "tell me" whether God was real. If anything, insofar that there wasn't any scientific evidence to definitively prove God, the logical position to adopt may indeed have been to declare that it's all superstitious fantasy. But through it all, my intuition was unequivocal: God exists. Paying it due attention then allowed me to see the limits of pure dialectic and having ultimately accepted its position on the matter, the implications eventually led to a complete transformation of my life.

Another instance of my intuition at work was in my grappling with the concept of countries, and specifically the view that countries were born from noble aspirations and motives. This didn't fit the trajectory of my overall position and my emotions strongly resisted the validity of it, but again it was my intuition that urged me to consider the idea, leading me to uncover a wealth of new perspectives as a result.

Therefore, similar to the feelings of dissatisfaction and unrest that I have singled out, I believe that following our intuition at any given moment is crucial if we are to grow towards becoming our true selves; indeed, I would even go as far as to say that the feelings of dissatisfaction are themselves a form of intuition. Thus our intuition is perhaps the closest thing to our true selves having a voice. If we choose to ignore it then we would in effect be ignoring ourselves, listening instead to something or someone else. Hence why it is unsurprising that in this domineering and power-hungry world, we are so often instructed away from following our intuition and taught to simply obey authorities and prescribed norms. To heed our own voice, therefore, requires great confidence and bravery and can very much feel like "me against the world." Though if my own experience has taught me anything, that is precisely what becoming the truth of oneself is.

Thirdly and finally, always remember that you were born to *live*. And this search for ourselves, to challenge the world, wake up to the power within, and thereby become who we truly are, is nothing less than life or death. To live according to the truth of ourselves is the only way to be fully *alive*, and any other life is not life at all, but death. As we shall see in the following chapters, however, it is a process against which there are undeniably powerful forces, seeking relentlessly to diminish and undermine. In this world, there exists a *system* designed to suppress and extirpate any knowledge or desire to realize ourselves; to shroud us in darkness and ignorance so that we do *not* make the choice to live according to the truth and simply remain in silent obedience. Choosing to defy all impositions and become none but oneself, therefore, is truly a revolutionary act. It is a restoration of sovereignty over our own lives, from the world, the system, and all its imposing structures, back to ourselves and the truth—to God.

Remember, no matter your origins or present circumstances, you were born into this world as *you*.

No one else, but *you*.

You are your most valuable asset, your greatest prize.
You are your most precious gift—to yourself and to *us*.

Your battles may be different from mine and the form of the struggle will vary from person to person, but the path to resolution is always the same.

All it takes is a choice.

The choice to be *me*. The choice to be free.

Part 2
Banned from Belonging
Conflict. Exile.

Chapter 7
Why Am I? Where Am I?

What is the truth?

In this world, most of us will believe ourselves to be free. We cannot see any chains or physical restraints to our choices or actions. Within the boundaries of our physical capacity and what we deem to be possible and correct, we presume that we can make any choice we wish and, indeed, our world operates on the basis that we are free and therefore responsible for the choices we make.

Certainly, there is no way to guarantee any outcome and it is not uncommon for the effects and ramifications of our actions to be at odds with our intention. But whether we reap the benefits of positive outcomes or pay the consequences for negative outcomes, we take it for granted that we were the agents who enacted the choice. Thus, unless demonstrable otherwise, we live under the presumption that we are free to do as we wish within the bounds of our respective capacities.

If there is a truth, therefore, *freedom* is one that we assume.

Based on the assumed truth of freedom, we can also infer that we each have the capability to shape our own lives through our choices and actions, though to what degree will differ depending on our access to resources and information, to name a couple of potential variables. Thus to compensate for any deficiencies, we can move to expand our capabilities individually but also collectively, that is, to cooperate with one another to achieve common aims. Working together, we are able to maximize our influence over our shared circumstances and better our individual lives.

Which begs the question: The world that we see around us, is it how we would wish?

Do our lives and the circumstances that we inhabit reflect who we are and satisfy our innermost yearnings?

Or do we have a sense, a feeling, a murmuring in our depth, telling us that something is amiss, that somehow our lives are not how they should be, how they need to be?

In asking the question, it must be stated that there is no "correct" answer. Some among us may be perfectly content with their lot, to simply watch the world go by as the planet keeps on turning. In keeping with the truth of freedom, to feel as such and make choices accordingly is certainly their prerogative. Yet for many, this privilege of comfort and satisfaction with the circumstances of themselves and the wider world is one that has not been afforded. In its stead, such individuals are saddled with an inexplicable feeling, a mysterious sense of unease that has been felt for what seems their entire lives. It is a yearning for something else—something *more*.

Guided by this feeling and in searching for answers, we might ask ourselves questions such as, Who am I? What am I? What do I want? We put ourselves under the microscope, examine ourselves through the prism of our questions. We attempt to comprehend the world we inhabit, the circumstances in which we are situated. But all the while, in the midst of our inquiry, *those* feelings grow stronger—

Dissatisfaction. Incompletion. Frustration. Unrest.

As these feelings grow more pressing, so does the urgency for answers.

Why do I feel this way?
Why am I in unrest?
Why am I?

Why?

But asking the question however repeatedly seems to bring us no closer to resolution. So eventually we change track, we shift our perspective. We now begin to question our very questioning, to ask why we are asking *why* to begin with. The answer would seem obvious; it is because we have these feelings—

Dissatisfaction. Incompletion. Frustration. Unrest.

But since asking why seems to lead to no answers, many among us simply learn to live with the feelings. We learn to accept them, to ignore them.

>To detach from the person feeling them.

>To detach from ourselves.

>To *kill* ourselves.

>Suicide.

—

This process of futile questioning and its ultimate, bitter end—suicide—is not, however, referring necessarily to the act of physically terminating one's life. It is rather the point at which we, convinced that there are no answers or, indeed, no purpose to the feelings of discontent, decide that we will heed them no further; to kill that part of us that prompts us to do so. We deal with a problem that has no perceivable solution by getting rid of the problem itself—*ourselves*—and continue to exist in the aftermath of this psychological suicide.

Exercising our freedom, it is we who make this choice. But should we investigate further into the death of ourselves, we might see that it isn't entirely self-committed, that there is an element of affliction, the fingerprints of another entity. If we look closer, if we look *wider,* we might see that behind every death, every suicide, there was a force that urged the act, a voice that whispered incitement, a temptation that beckoned us to fall.

What is being said here?

That perhaps, there is some *thing,* some *one* that makes us kill ourselves, that tells us our feelings of unease and discontent towards this world, ourselves, and the lives that we live are not to be heeded. More, that these feelings are our fault, our problem, that we are to blame, and that we must *kill* to rid ourselves of them—kill ourselves, for the feelings are inseparable from ourselves. We don't know what these feelings are, but we know we must kill ourselves to kill them.

We know, because we are told.

Just as I have these feelings, deep within myself I sense a force, I hear a voice that tells me the feelings must be silenced and put to death. I am ordered by a command that tells me the feelings must be killed—if I am to act, if I am to work, if I am to belong.

To do as the world says, to work as society tells me, to belong among *them*.

For I am told these feelings of mine are incompatible with *them*—the former must die if I am to be a part of the latter. If I am to operate among *them*, these feelings of mine which would appear to separate me from *them*, cannot survive. There are no two ways. The choice must be made, the deed must be done. If you want *them*, the feelings must be killed.

You must die.

With each passing day, the command to kill grows stronger while our feelings wither and fade; each moment in this world is a step closer in the long, escorted walk towards the gallows. Until one day, at the chime of the bell, we arrive at the point of judgment.

Hooded, blinded, gagged, and bound; in total darkness, there is nothing further to see, nowhere now to run or hide; no further chance to speak.

It is time, to make a choice.

A noose around your neck, a knife in your hands, a gun against your head. With all other voices drowned away, in your head there is nothing but the sound of *them*, inviting, enticing, screaming—

Die. Kill. Murder.

The sands of time are quickly running low, and there is nothing left to do now but jump with the noose, to wield the knife against yourself, to pull the trigger of the gun pointed at your head. The time has come for *me* to die and be rid of myself, to extinguish the last and already atrophied vestiges of *those* feelings and to be filled instead with *them*. This is the moment where I cease to live as *I* and begin to exist among *them*.

This is the moment for me to become *them*.

Gently beckoned by the strange illusion of what seems to await beyond the abyss—belonging, identity, purpose, recognition, approval, security—we are convinced. This life, to be sure, is nothing much to lose. Indeed, what is there to lose but these troublesome feelings with the nagging discomfort and obstruction that they constantly induce? Further, was it not *them* who have been calling for the whole duration of life thus far, and towards *them* that you have been walking? To arrive at this point, to make the choice, to lose yourself and become *them*—this is where the road ends. This is the goal, the aim, the final destination. All that remains is to make the choice.

Die. Kill. Murder.

But it is then, in the second before suicide and as you fleetingly ponder on the feelings one last time, that by some miracle or divine intervention, the realization hits you: these feelings, they belong to you. More than that, the feelings *are* you.

They are *you*.

The dissatisfaction, the sense of incompletion, frustration, and unrest that you felt all along—these were not imperfections to be denied, inconveniences to be silenced, or defects to be fixed. They were in fact warnings—guides—to be heeded and followed. They were *I* calling out to me, messages from my depth compelling me to survive. To *live*.

To live as *I* would.

Within myself, there is conflict. There is a struggle, a battle, between surrender and confrontation, pacifism and resistance, suicide and survival—between evil and good. I am the battleground for this war, and the only thing that lies between the two—between life and death—is a choice.

I am the one who chooses the victor.

The outcome will be decided by me.

Indeed, the noose is around *my* neck, the knife in *my* hands, the gun against *my* head. I have the choice, the power, to determine whether I live or die. And having now recognized the truth of freedom and the power to choose, for the first time I recognize the thought and the option—the *possibility*—that I might live as *I*. But with this newfound discovery comes also the discernment of something more sinister inside myself, something that has sought ever so subtly to lead me astray and to push me to use this power of choice against myself—to choose to *kill* myself.

Faced with this ominous entity, I sense, with no other way to describe it, that I am hated.

Something hates me and my will to live as myself. It is something indescribable, something unspeakable, something terrible. It is a hatred that seems to have been active for my entire life, working incessantly from the shadows to turn me away from myself, to have me hate myself, and thereby snuff out any desire for a life and a world that is in any way an expression of *me*. In very real terms, this hatred opposes life—and not merely in the sense of death, but of *murder*. It is that which kills life, kills what would have me live as *I*—my identity, my uniqueness, my *spirit*—and indeed, it is such that compels me to do the killing myself.

It is hatred as anti-life; it is "live" inverted and reversed—it is evil.

And it is within me, operating under the guise of myself to sabotage in stealth.

It is the enemy within, the adversary of the mind and spirit.

It is the Devil.

Where is this enemy, this evil, from? How did it get here?

Why is it here, inside myself? And most crucially of all, why does it want *me* to be silenced, to be killed?

All of a sudden, the questions are not asked to the feelings anymore; the finger of blame no longer points towards what I now know is myself. The enemy has been identified, and it is not these feelings that dissuade me from settling, urging me instead to seek further and search deeper—to look *wider*.

I finally see: the enemy is not *I*.

Rather, the enemy is that which seeks to destroy *I* and silence that which supports its promulgation. And now that we know our enemy, our gaze fixated on the darkness that it is, we begin to recognize everything around us that has been built to crush our self-belief and confidence, to diminish the power of choice that we have over ourselves and blind us from the truth—the truth of freedom, and the power to choose *I* thereupon. Instead, we see a world that seeks to have me use this power and truth against myself, to turn ourselves against ourselves to push another agenda. We start to discern a structure that is designed to replace *I* with *them*, and to have us be vassals—slaves—to priorities and purposes that not only neglect, but actively negate the advancement of our spirit, and the nurturing of our happiness thereby.

And why?

Because to be *me*, to be *you*, to be *us*, means to not be *them*. If I am living as *I* would, it is a zero-sum outcome; I can no longer live under the dictates of *them*. And in this world that seeks imposition, suppression of expression, and thereby the production of outcomes solely for the benefit of *them*, this cannot be. It will not be tolerated, and by all means, it will be stamped out and extinguished.

> In this world, I cannot be free.
> I cannot be *me*.

Now that we know, we begin to see—

A world of evil, of deceit, created to blind us from the truth.

A structure of control, built to imprison our minds and suffocate our spirit.

Now that we know, we finally see.

We see *the system*.

Let us ask that question again: What is the truth?

As we have established, we can meaningfully assume the truth of our freedom, that is, our ability to make any choice we wish within the boundaries of our individual capacity. It was also inferred thereupon that we, both individually and collectively, possess the capability to shape our lives through our choices and actions.

Yet having delved into the feelings of dissatisfaction and having subsequently discerned forces that seek to have us use our freedom against ourselves, we are confronted with a disconcerting paradox: that coexistent with the truth of our freedom is the truth of our slavery.

We live in a world where despite the truth of freedom, we are not exercising our power of choice for the expression and betterment of *I* but instead serving opposing interests only to the advantage of *them*. We are indeed slaves, and deep within ourselves, we know it; we *feel* it—

Dissatisfaction. Incompletion. Frustration. Unrest.

How did this come to be? In spite of the truth of freedom, how can we be slaves?

Why are we in bondage?

Upon the truth of both—that is, of freedom and of slavery— the answer is clear and can only be thus: we *choose* to be slaves.

Over freedom, we have chosen enslavement.
Over life, we have chosen death.
Over *I*, we have chosen *them*.

But do we do so willingly? Or are we somehow manipulated, coerced? For if I knew my own freedom—if I knew the truth—

why would I willingly choose to serve interests that negate *I* and my fulfillment therein? Further, if I knew that I was a slave—if I knew the truth—why would I willingly choose to remain in enslavement?

Why would I choose *them* over *I*—indeed, over *us*?

The answer, it would appear, lies in the question: we would choose to serve *I* if we knew we were free to do so. We would no longer choose to be slaves if we knew we were enslaved.

Thus we would choose—*if* we knew.

But it seems we are instead in ignorance.
Somehow unconscious, oblivious, asleep.

What, then, keeps us from knowing? What keeps us in darkness? What blinds us to this multifaceted truth that we are kept in bondage despite being free? What so pacifies us, leads us astray, that we would willingly exercise our freedom to choose enslavement?

A person, a mind, that is free by definition cannot be subjugated. Such a being would exercise his or her freedom under all circumstances, always at the discretion of his or her true nature, who he or she truly is, and what best serves the cause of his or her identity. But since we do not seem to live in such a way—that is, in a manner expressive of our respective uniqueness and that creates a world reflective of *us*—a certain question presents itself:

Could it be that we are in fact *not* free?

Could it be that we are indeed slaves, and that the reason we do not fight our enslavement is because we *think* we are free?

Could it be that we live under merely the pretense of freedom—*false* freedom—thus keeping us from awakening to this reality?

Could it be that the device that this world and the system use to maintain our captivity is the *perception* of freedom itself, the illusion of choice?

Could it be?

The question, upon being asked, suggests the possibility and allows us to see a new reality. Despite our freedom, we are born slaves for we are born into this system, with its mark pressed deep within our psyche. The system has conditioned and imprisoned our minds to make us unaware of our captivity, thus to free ourselves from our predicament is not seen as a requirement or indeed an option. For although the feelings of dissatisfaction arise in response to our enslavement to tell us something is deeply wrong, we are deceived and made blind to the truth of our slavery by the system's hypnosis.

Thus we point the finger of blame towards ourselves.
To rid us of these feelings, we proceed to *kill* ourselves.

The system is built upon our deaths—we kill the feelings, the compulsion to live as ourselves. Over and over again we kill *I*, and it is upon our psychological suicide that the system stands.

It is a system of death, designed to inculcate our minds with fear and to reject our desire to live as *I*, to have us kill ourselves so that the system lives in our place.

We are enslaved by the system, held in bondage as a result of having killed ourselves by the system's incitement. We have vacated sovereignty over ourselves and have allowed the system to fill the void; we have ceased to live as *I* and have instead become extensions of the system, existing solely to fulfill its bidding. Duped and beguiled by the system's manipulation, we have created circumstances of *exile* in which we are alienated from our true selves. Living in such a world we are in continuous unrest, but being blind to our condition and not knowing why, we are doomed to repeat the psychological suicide that tightens the system's grip over our lives, thereby perpetuating our misery.

Let us now proceed to explore some of the system's key pillars and the mechanisms by which it debilitates our minds. It will quickly become apparent that despite the insidiousness of its methods, the system itself is in plain sight.

It is all around us and, indeed, within us all.

Chapter 8
Politics

What is the essence of politics? One word: power.

More specifically, it is the power associated with human relations, often conflated with governance, and the ability to overtly or covertly regulate the behavior of others and mold a shared society according to the views, priorities, and needs of those wielding power.

In the same vein, what is the essence of a political system? It is a framework or structure in which this relational power among humans is attained, maintained, arranged, and exchanged in a given society.

And in our current age, the prevailing order is that of democracy, a category of a political system that vests political power unto the *demos*, that is, the "people," a body of individuals each endowed with the ability to influence the application of power within their society. For many, it is the political system held up as the ideal, the most conducive to freedom and the power of choice for the greatest number. But a curious quirk of our time is the concept of *representative* democracy, whereby the people in their multitudes do not exercise power for themselves but instead are made responsible for electing *representatives* who are entrusted to make decisions on their behalf, supposedly with their best interests in mind. It is said to be through such a process that we have a voice, that we are heard in chambers of power. It is they who become our voice and through them as our vassals that we are heard.

But are we?

It is important to remember that in a representative democracy, there is no specific mechanism to guarantee that representatives will actually represent and wield power for the collective benefit of the people, as determined by the people themselves. We supposedly trust that they will, based on whatever promises and programs they have offered. And if a given representative is deemed by the people to have done a bad job at representing their interests and welfare, then it is said the people can "punish" the representative in the next election by electing an alternative candidate, who, through a lengthy and often expensive process of campaigning, has convinced enough hearts and minds among the demos that he or she will do better. This entire framework is intended to ensure that the people are in charge based on their power to elect and eject, and the representatives the ones to listen to and obey the people.

But do they?

Considering the all-encompassing nature of issues currently facing the world and the growing potential for every life to be impacted by the actions (or lack thereof) taken to address them, it is perhaps one of the most pertinent and necessary questions of our time: Among our elected representatives, is the voice of the demos heard? Is the will of the people obeyed?

Do our representatives *actually* represent us?

For though some have good intentions (and many do not), there is a conspicuous disquiet among the peoples of major representative democracies about the inability of representatives to deliver on the changes they wish to see and the obstacles that interfere with even sincere efforts to attain them. While the importance of representatives acting decisively and virtuously grows in proportion to the scale of the world's issues, more than ever it would appear they are stuck in inaction, with the people equally divided and societies becoming less and less hospitable and reflective all the while.

Indeed, in these circumstances, it often seems that representatives just do what they want or, more specifically, do the bidding of the rich and powerful—the elites—while the people simply suffer what they must. The collective wishes of the demos, even for the demographic whose preferred candidate is in power, are not the agenda, and the voice of the ordinary person simply goes unheard, unanswered. As this problem grows ever clearer, however, it is important to again remember that our representatives, once in power, are bound to nothing that necessitates them to exercise their decision-making according to the benefit and priorities of the demos. That certainly may be the job description and thereby the duty, but, to say again, never in systems of representative democracy is it a necessity.

As representatives increasingly seem willing to exploit this democratic loophole, the sense among the people that the world around them is not what they asked for, that the circumstances they find themselves in are not where they want to be, that their lives do not represent who they are, multiplies and festers. Indeed, as a collective, they increasingly become agitated by those familiar feelings—

Dissatisfaction. Incompletion. Frustration. Unrest.

Compelled by these feelings for something more, something *better*, it is perhaps a rather strange state of affairs, then, that the demos would continually try to seek a solution in politics, that is, through this system and those who present themselves as representatives to wield power within it, despite what would seem the consistent failure of politics as such to deliver a resolution.

Why is it that the people collectively continue to look to political and electoral action—debating, fundraising, canvassing, voting, petitioning, and occasionally demonstrating—to address the problems they see? Does the demos somehow continue to believe that the system, at its core, has the capacity to serve their collective interests? And on the basis of this enduring faith, do they somehow believe it is simply a case of one more election, one more vote, to have their voices heard and for "change" to be delivered? Is it an unspoken assumption among the people that it is through the system, and simply the "right" candidate among aspiring representatives, that better days are to come?

If the trajectory of recent times is anything to go by, it

would seem this hope for deliverance by the system of representative democracy has largely been in vain or worse, manipulated and misused. Election after election, one representative after another, it would seem merely to be the same cycle of unfulfilled promises, empty words, deceit, and subsequent despair. And through it all, the people continue to participate in the system, seemingly with no choice or solution other than to look to representatives and the system as it currently stands. What keeps the demos so fixated as such, despite what should be by now insurmountable proof of ineptitude, failure, and even malevolence? What compels them to persist in such a pathological and ultimately fruitless engagement? It is often said that the definition of insanity is to repeat the same thing, over and over again, and expect different results. On these grounds, as a collective decision-making body, has the demos proven itself to be insane?

Insane—or rather, trapped?

Trapped, captured, and ensnared in a quagmire system, one that intends to produce helplessness and seeks deliberately to subjugate and imprison?

For even as we lament the mournful condition of the demos, the sense of injustice is perhaps born primarily from the idea that the people are in charge, the expectation that decisions *should* be taken for their collective benefit. Indeed, more than anything, it is perhaps faith in this expectation that leads the people to persevere in its toxic relationship with the representative system. If it were the case, however, and today's systems of representative democracies are designed in such a way to serve the collective will of the people, then should we not be seeing at least some tangible evidence of deliverance?

Yet with the continuous march to centralize power into fewer and fewer hands, the rapidly widening gulf of wealth between the ultrarich and everybody else, the growing intrusion of the state into the everyday lives of people, the incessant lying and misleading of populations by authorities, the deterioration of healthcare or a total lack thereof despite bloated taxation and expenditure, and the ever-present threat of a nuclear catastrophe, one would not be hard-pressed to entertain the thought that this is in fact *not* the case. That in reality, the system of representative democracy does *not* work to represent the people, that it is geared to marginalize the people and undermines their interests for the sake of representatives themselves or those they *actually* represent. Indeed, viewed through this lens, the deterioration we see unfolding around us would begin to make some semblance of sense.

Take, for instance, the primary and most fundamental power granted to the demos, that of electoral choice. While this power (often referred to as a right) is the hallmark of representative democracy and fiercely defended as the prize of hard-won victories against certain power-hoarding groups, its principal function is merely transference, that is, simply the selection of who the demos vests its power unto. And its efficacy as the *self-expression* of the people, that is, as a choice that most closely resembles that which they agree is their collective will, is greatly or even fatally diminished when, in the vast majority of instances, the pool of candidates from which the people choose is one into which they have had little to no input. This is to say nothing of what the candidates stand for in terms of policy, where for any areas that they are all in agreement, the choice for any alternative approaches are removed entirely for those matters.

Take next the power of ratification, to deliberate on a particular proposition between a given set of options (in the form of a referendum, for example). Here again, we see the same shortcoming, with the framing of options simply dictated to the people by representatives who, for one reason or another, wish to shift the onus of decision-making onto the people.

In such a light, it is certainly understandable if the people feel disaffected by the politics of today, and these powers to elect and ratify come across to them as somewhat invalid—farcical, even. Though it is certainly true that representative democracy provides what seem to be avenues of choice and participation—something other political systems perhaps do not—the scope and significance of what is granted become meager, to say the least, when the options from which the people are able to choose are invariably treated, limited, and constrained.

On these grounds already, the people are more accurately described not as *voters*, with the means to meaningfully participate in the representative system as a democracy, but rather as mere *consumers*, endorsing or rejecting certain choices and options over others within already predetermined bounds.

Delving further, we find that this malaise is compounded by the media machine that acts as the primary disseminator of information and opinion for those among the people who are politically oriented. In the established *news* media, though the spectrum of opinion is seemingly wide from left to right, the message is treated and packaged within the same basic framework of assumptions, and certain fundamentals remain unquestioned, not least the structure of representation.

The vast majority of news media engages with political issues, questions, and all the real-life consequences that unfold from their outcome almost invariably within the language of the representative system and its practices—what representatives are doing or saying, what they are planning, why, what they should do or say, and which representative or group of representatives should be supported based on all this. Even seemingly apolitical matters are by and large framed and discussed in these terms. The news media has its gaze firmly fixed on *them*—and with the news media as their eyes, the political class among the people does also.

A primary consequence of this is the limiting of the scope of debate and thereby the boundaries of thought and possibility. When the bulk of news content, especially with regards to societal problems and issues, is focused almost entirely on the actions and words of representatives, it has the effect of relegating the people themselves out of the equation, since the natural assumption becomes one of "they're in charge" and "they'll do something about it." Within the minds of the people, it is the representatives and leaders who take center stage, at the expense of the people themselves. The constriction of choice in the voting process is thus further exacerbated by this psychological disempowerment, with the social change required for perceived problems and issues being inevitably outsourced to representatives.

And yet the problem goes further. Through the seeming disregard for genuine inquiry into current affairs and views pertaining to them, the so-called mainstream news media induces a narrowness of mind that is becoming increasingly obvious and widespread. Nowadays there is an increasingly alarming tendency to focus merely on portrayal, whereby outlets report any developments solely in a manner that is conducive and comfortable to their particular ideological leaning, with very little consideration or respect for contrasting perspectives. In such a climate, "facts" are turned to weapons aimed at denigrating others, voiced by "experts" who corroborate only the dominant view, thus reinforcing the depiction of "the other" as wrong, ignorant, and in many cases dangerous. Meaningfully informing audiences so that they might understand a situation, formulate their own views, and consider a variety of positions on it is clearly no longer sought by the majority of news media. Rather, the intent seems merely to label and exclude, to portray a given circumstance, event, or people as *this* and no further. Indeed, the chasm of division that is apparent among the political class of the demos today can to a large extent be attributed to the nature of "news" as such.

Turning our attention also to the section of the demos outside of the political class, that is, those individuals who are unaware and unconcerned with what is going on beyond their immediate perceptions, we see the media play an equally insidious role in the marginalization of the people, albeit in different categories. Among such elements of the people, we see an interaction primarily with social media, sport, consumerism, and various forms of "trash" media and the tabloid press, all of which serve as a distraction from the act of thinking itself, let alone defining boundaries for thought. Indeed, it is by distracting and thereby diminishing the ability of the people to think that allows them to be simply ignored for the most part but steered to make purely emotional responses to political issues when called upon, say, in times of an election or referendum. Indeed, it is via the social, tabloid, and trash media themselves that the people will be driven to act as such, with their tendency to distill often complex topics to one-liner soundbites and provocative imagery to trigger irrational impulses.

Driven by their relative disinterest and taken for a ride by the media in this respect, vast numbers among the people are either utterly sidelined or tragically manipulated. Among the political class of the people also, the unwillingness of the news media to question and hold not just individual representatives and their parties but the system in its entirety to account largely denies them the means to inform themselves effectively, the critical first step upon which they might then organize in such a way that actively influences and controls decision making.

Clearly, however, the damaging effects of the media combined with the built-in limitations to the people's power to choose would make it appear as though meaningful participation of the people is *not* wanted, indeed, that it is even deliberately denied, as if to suggest it is not the purpose of the people to do so.

In a democracy, it is the people who are in charge, and the representatives must listen to and obey the people!—so it is believed.

Yet very much to the contrary, it is clear we do not control our representatives or so-called leaders, but rather that they control us. When electoral choice is simply selecting from options already determined and the means for the people to adequately inform themselves and thereby circumvent the restrictions are effectively absent, then the choice that the people believe they have in representative democracies is illusory and the freedom they consider themselves to have merely a perception. But convinced that they are free and in charge, the people will continue to divest their power through the representative system and generate legitimacy for policies and options that are not for them, in their interests, or supportive of their well-being.

Herein we find the actual purpose of the people within our systems of representative democracy. That is, rather than to build a world for themselves through the enacting of meaningful choices, the purpose of the people is to elevate and sustain the class of political masters set above them, to be exploited and utilize their power of agency to justify choices that build only a world for *them*. The people, then, are not partners in power but merely a source of it, an unwitting support for control and authority.

The purpose of the people, evidently, is to be enslaved.

This all begs one certain question: From whence comes this system of representation? I say, it is born from the concept of countries, that given geographical areas of this globe be fenced off and bounded by borders, and within these borders, a *state* and *government* be installed as the entity to implement rules and organize the society under which the people exist. The concept of countries is a tool for and of states, and that countries be run by a state and government is perhaps one of the most basic, fundamental, and unquestioned assumptions among the people. Indeed, it is the only world that we have ever known. Representative democracy itself is the product of the evolution of state systems, burgeoning out from rebellions against monarchs and princely castes exercising absolute rule. But to the present day, what we see is the assumption of countries as a nation-state, requiring to be unified, monolithic blocs functioning and moving under the direction of a state, that is, the assumption of governments and citizens, rulers and subjects—masters and slaves.

In the context of countries and national borders, the masters (governments, in more politically correct terms) use their political power to decide policy and law, and this is applied to all within the borders of the country. In representative democracies, winning an election gives a representative or their party the right to impose their program on the entirety of the people, and thus politics by a government, representative or otherwise, is necessarily a form of *imposition*. And so the concept of countries, in addition to breeding an alienating mentality of separation—*here* and *there*, *us* and *them*—also sows division among the people *within* national borders as a result; the people label one another enemies and betrayers precisely because of the prospect of imposition. For the demographic whose preferred candidate or party has lost, power under the guise of popular support is used to force unto them an agenda that they have neither chosen nor agreed to.

While countries, representative politics, and the principle of imposition are an unmistakable cause of strife among the people in this regard, the more hidden and perhaps greatest danger of representative systems is the risk—or rather, reality—of permanent state machinery and public institutions being hijacked by malign outside influences, most often in the form of private corporations and foreign states. For while there is no mechanism to guarantee that elected representatives and governments will work on the people's behalf, what we so often see are states acting in ways to actively undermine the public, to structure and arrange societies of entire nations in a way that advances only narrow special interests.

The forms in which this phenomenon manifests can vary. Most commonly, third-party actors make governmental representatives beholden to their financial or media backing (often both), compelling political authorities to wield power to suit the needs of their sponsors above all. And equally if not more commonplace, is for those who occupy positions of power in the state, government, and major private organizations to be cut from the same cloth in terms of attitudes and ways of thinking.

Compared to the former practice, the latter reality may come across as less outwardly corrupt, but they are inextricably linked insofar that an openness among government representatives to unscrupulous private solicitation requires a mutual disregard for the public interest. It is a tendency born from significant elements within the ruling classes in both public and private spheres embodying the same fundamental beliefs that are inherently self-absorbed, elitist, and domineering, assuming that people are required or, indeed, that it is their very purpose, to be managed and herded towards decided objectives.

It does not require leaps of the imagination to see how this undermines the creation of a society expressive of the people's collective wishes and interests. For insofar that the representative system, by its very nature, inhibits meaningful participation of the people, the ruling class will, by *its* very nature, mold and maneuver a given society with selfish intent, thereby creating a world that is reflective not of *us*, but of *them*, diametrically opposed to one based on the individuality and uniqueness of each person and the ability for each to realize their destiny therein.

With the established media having become a key component of the dominant ruling class, the media then actively participates in this process to actualize a world solely for *them*, with developments and steps taken to this end either whispered quietly, going unreported entirely, or worse, packaged and propagated to the people as *for their own good*. The established media thus serves as a loyal and indispensable interface between self-serving rulers and their perceived slaves—us—administering a devitalizing poison and starving the people of truth, robbing them of their ability to make meaningful choices so that they might live unto themselves.

> That word has come before us once again: truth.
> What is the truth?

> It is clear: representation does not represent you.
> Representative leaders, representative democracy, the representative system—none of it.

> It cannot, for the truth is that only you can represent yourself.

> It is you who will create your life and you who will change your circumstances. That these will and must come from another—from *them*—is the lie.

> It is a lie that surrenders all power, all freedom, to *them*.
> It is a lie that enslaves us to *them*.
> Yet it is a lie we the people believe.

And it is through belief in this lie that the modern mind, captured and made blind by politics and the representative system, relegates the people themselves—you and me—from the realm of possibilities. For insofar that the people themselves are exiled from the imagination and power continues to be yielded, never can we say we have attained a *democracy*, that is, power in the hands of the people to realize their own destiny, without the coercion and imposition of a state or government acting in the name of "representation."

So I urge you, resolve at once to take direct and personal action toward individual emancipation, to assume the mantle of leadership to your own life, to reject *them* as your masters and yourself as their slave. Further, we are under constant siege by forces seeking to exploit representation to manipulate society for narrow, selfish advantages, at the expense of the people. We must therefore remain vigilant, educate ourselves, hone our awareness, and *engage* with the system and all its corruptions, since with your consent or without, politics will impose itself upon you. And when our striving for self-determination and emancipation is thus threatened, there must be resistance through organized dissidence.

For I say again: the answer to change in your life lies not with *them* and the system.

All the power that you have chosen to vest unto *them*, vest unto yourself.

The power that you have ceded to *them*, take it back.

Look unto yourself, for the power is in your hands.

All it takes is a choice.

But alas, it is a choice that we all too often do not make. Indeed, one that we somehow seem unable to make. Why might this be?

Perhaps because it was not taught to us; because we did not learn it in school.

Chapter 9
School

Education, as is commonly known, means to "draw out." But to draw out what? Presumably, whatever is inside the one being educated. And what lies within?

The answer, clearly, does not come from biology but from all those intangible aspects that manifest themselves in behavior and drive a person to create their tangible reality. Namely, we are referring to thoughts, character, instincts, talents, strengths, weaknesses, perspective—the list goes on, and there is no single word to neatly explain or summarize what lies within except that it is *the person him or herself*, with all the culture, the whole world, the entire universe, that constitutes everything that makes this person who they are.

To "draw out," then, means to bring forth *the person within*— the total and absolute uniqueness within each one of us, who we really are, who we are born to be, indeed, the only person we can ever truly be—ourselves.

The purpose of education, therefore, in the truest sense of the word, is to help us *become ourselves*. To this end, there might be a multitude of different methods, philosophies, tools, and ways of organizing, but in order to qualify as education, the central and most fundamental mission must be the same—to draw out the person within.

And in our current societies, the place most commonly attended to receive an education is *school*, and it is often mandated by law that children of a certain age attend school or be educated at home or elsewhere along the lines determined by the school system. Indeed, the standard perception is to conflate the two, that school *is* education, that without attending school or having followed the school system, children are not considered "educated."

Which begs the key question: Does school educate?

Let us, however, first take a moment to explore what such an education would look like—what school perhaps should be like—based on an understanding of education as described above.

Consider the nature of a child, say between the ages of two to seven. During this point in a child's life, what we see is the purest demonstration of a child's instincts for creativity and curiosity. Children, especially in their formative years, are innately predisposed to *absorption* and *expression*; they are insatiably curious about the world around them—seeking to learn and absorb—whilst simultaneously they are unstoppable in their desire to create and express themselves, that is, to release and project their inner world unto the world around them. Children are perhaps, in this respect, the most perfect encapsulations of the fundamental duality of human nature, that is, to give and receive.

Granted, it may often appear as if children's "expression" is simply to run amok at random and on impulse, and for this preoccupation to completely drown out any inkling of curiosity in the workings of the world around them. Yet if we consider the child's activity to be its expression, then it is not by any means something we should perceive as a nuisance and therefore suppress; rather, it must be utilized, configured, and directed for positive and productive results. And if the child is up to no good—as is sometimes the case—then certainly it is a matter of intervening to create circumstances for constructive activity. Whichever it may be, what is of crucial importance is to encourage activity on the part of the child and to allow it to flourish, thus giving the child motive to demand and absorb information and to provide context and relevance to the imparted knowledge thereby.

It is herein that lies the foremost role of a *teacher*—to harness the intense activity of the child (or create circumstances for useful activity), to instruct on its basis, and give it direction through leadership and discipline to produce growth. Indeed, an education with a child's activity—the child's *life*—as its starting point and center,[6] with teachers instructing in a manner that is contextual and relevant to the child would encourage the child's desire to express whilst simultaneously cultivating its curiosity, thus unifying its two foremost instincts.

Such an education surely offers the child the best chance to grow with balance and produce the most exquisite synergy

---

[6] This emphasis on the need for the child's life to be the focus of education is expounded by John Dewey in his *The School and Society: Being Three Lectures* (1899), specifically in the second lecture: *The School and the Life of the Child*

between the two instincts to express and absorb. Indeed, we may witness the child eventually combine the foundation of knowledge and discipline received during childhood and adolescence with a harnessing of its confidence for expression to create new worlds for itself, that is, to expand the boundaries of what is currently known and push the limits of what is thought possible. Furthermore, education as such will develop our greatest natural advantage as a species: cooperation. It will help the child understand through experience that no one exists in isolation, that together we are stronger, that we are more than the sum of parts. Learning cooperation, children will experience the power of mutual support, and becoming adults, their ability to work collectively at the peak of their mental, physical, and creative capacities will surely unleash levels of innovation and progress never before witnessed.

Idealistic (or naive, some may argue) though this may be, what is being described here is education that is, put simply, centered on the child itself. Its foremost aim would be to do what education is supposed to do, that is, to draw out what is within the child; to instruct based on the child's activity and experience, whilst nurturing the confidence to express their inner world in a disciplined and purposeful manner; in short, to develop the *person* of the child, guided by the understanding that it is the uniqueness within that is the child's greatest asset and contribution and thus our most valued treasure.

This then begs the key question once again: Does school, as we now envisage education to be, actually educate?

To be sure, education as we traditionally understand it today, in the sense of the state-sponsored public school system, was developed and proliferated in tandem with the rise of modern nation-states and the need for states to breed a standardized citizenry for greater social cohesion.[7] While this purpose certainly remains, however, what is more conspicuous nowadays as the school system's *raison d'être* is to meet the needs of an industrialized economy, that is, to supply industry and businesses with a steady stream of workers.

Indeed, the path of life as such is so obvious, so ordinary, so taken for granted, that upon finishing school, the next question automatically asked is "Which job do I take?" or "Where can I work?" Getting a job is assumed to be the natural next step after school, that one went to school *for the express purpose* of getting a job. Thus from the very outset, it is clear the purpose of the school system is not to educate according to its true definition, and its primary function to supply industry with workers inexorably shapes the content of the school system and the treatment of those partaking within it.

For instance, there is a clear hierarchy within the subjects taught at school with so-called "STEM" (science, technology, engineering, and mathematics) subjects at the top, gradually cascading down to more deprioritized, even stigmatized, subjects such as social sciences, languages, literature, humanities, arts, and physical education. Needless to say, this hierarchy is invented purely because the STEM subjects are what modern industry most demands, and therefore the pursuit of them is most likely to lead to a job. However, it shouldn't require even a minute to see why

---

[8] This view has been expressed by critics of the modern public school system such as H.L. Mencken and John Taylor Gatto, among others. However, pioneers of the system such as Horace Mann and Henry Barnard made clear their admiration for the school system developed by the Prussian state during the 18th century, which utilized public education as a means to enhance state influence.

this mindset is critically flawed (at least in the context of the true definition of education), based on the simple reason that most children—most people, in fact—are either uninterested in STEM subjects or not intellectually predisposed to them. Yet by establishing a hierarchy of subjects, the school system automatically creates a hierarchy of value, in which a small minority of pupils are placed on a pedestal with others seen as having fewer prospects simply for their inability to perform according to imposed expectations.

What this tells us, essentially, is that the school system is not interested in fostering a diversity of talents, curiosities, or interests of students based on who they are. For a school system centered on the needs of industry, prioritizing a narrow spectrum of "core" subjects over others through timetabling, funding, and general attitude is logical and sensible, for pushing the needs of industry by its available means is what school is *supposed* to do.

But although *what* schools teach and the bias found therein can go some distance in revealing the motive and function of the school system, it is still perhaps secondary to *how* schools teach and indeed *why* the given methods and approaches are adopted.

Earlier it was mentioned that children are by instinct highly disposed to creativity and curiosity and that this manifests in their natural inclination for expression and absorption. What we see with the school system, however, is a particular, almost exclusive appeal to the latter of these instincts, with almost everything about the school environment geared towards merely the receiving of information, for listening and absorbing. Children and adolescents in school are largely treated as empty vessels needing to be filled, to accumulate information, and finally to reproduce what has been taught. Very little of school is intended to encourage activity and expression—indeed, expression *as and through* activity—and very seldom does it subsequently occur. If at all it does, it is most likely *despite* the school curriculum and not because of it, for instance, by the hand of an enlightened and charismatic teacher who is prepared to stray from the usual norms and boundaries.

This point is of particular importance since we know children's behavior—and that of people generally—is an expression and communication of who they are; that is, what they do and how they behave is a tangible projection of their inner world unto the world without. It is no less how we perceive them as people; without their expression or with the suppression of it, the person ceases to exist and be alive as themselves. It is tantamount to denying the distinct individual a release, and the prolonged enforcement of such treatment eventually will see the child disengage from their person within, to lose sight of and detach from their identity and uniqueness of character. And yet we see a school system that conspires against active expression and instead promotes obedience, subordination, and passivity. Some systems even go to such lengths as to invent epidemics of psychological illness to justify the administering of chemical anesthetics, in order to artificially pacify and suppress the activity of a child who cannot "sit still" through school.

Further, we find that the emphasis on passivity and the stifling of expression is fundamentally isolating. By inhibiting the natural inclination to convey themselves and the desire to associate with one another—all eyes fixed on the teacher, the board, the textbook, the test—school reduces students to partitioned components, and mutual assistance, rather than being fostered as the most natural way to achieve and find value as a cooperative whole (as is the case in *real life*), is instead incriminated and forbidden. Communing with one's peers is relegated only to the playground, building a conception among the child and adolescent that work is essentially solitary, and the aforementioned sense that more is accomplished together, that we are greater than the sum of parts, is lost.

Further still, school not only atomizes students to inhibit cooperation but actively seeks to drive them apart through the promotion of competition. When the primary form of assessment is individual testing, with grades and performance as a solitary effort determining places for the best schools and highest prizes, assisting peers becomes an act of self-harm and the failure of others something to logically hope for in order to advance oneself. Not stopping at passivity and subordination, the school system thereby destroys the natural will to cooperate and support, inducing instead a malignant selfishness among its participants to get ahead even at the cost of others. Indeed, this rotten tendency then becomes apparent in all areas of human society as children and adolescents seeking to undermine one another grow into adults, taking positions within businesses, organizations, governments, and states.

A word now must be said on the topic of individual testing, for herein do we see further corrupting effects of the school system on the character of students. To be specific, the primary means of assessment in the vast majority of school systems today is individual, *standardized* testing, that is, all students provided with the same information and all students assessed in their ability to reproduce this information according to a uniform, standardized measure and indeed under strict conditions of silent isolation. With seemingly ever-increasing emphasis placed on such tests and many societies treating them as the be-all and end-all to determine students' ability and subsequent life prospects, it is a growing and critical issue that vast numbers of children and adolescents are being labeled (and labeling themselves) as unintelligent and unworthy due to their inability to achieve within a narrow, unnatural mold.

However, standardized testing models can prove to be more subtle and insidious in their harm, stemming from the idea that all subjects—even the arts, where expression and thus subjectivity is perhaps the whole point—can and must be evaluated according to the criteria of a "standard" that is decided and imposed from above, by the system itself. Thus the end to which students work and judge themselves is not who they are and how best this person can be actualized, but instead, how closely they meet the imposed standard. Obedience, the repetition of instruction, fear of the wrong answer, thinking and acting only within defined limits—these become the dominant traits students grow to embody and those by which the system discriminates and selects. Their conception of achievement and value inevitably become tied not to their identity but to the demands of authority. What is most important is not *who I am*, but rather how well I know what I'm told to know, do what I'm told to do, and say what I'm told to say.

Let us now ask ourselves the key question one final time: Does school educate?

Based even on our brief exploration, it would appear school is not interested in education, for the simple fact that school is not interested in people and the process of drawing out the person within. Its foremost concern and purpose seems rather to be a distinct and malevolent form of socialization, molding the minds of children and adolescents not to become themselves, but always to meet the needs of something other than themselves—of industry, of society, of the system.

It is, therefore, clear: school does not educate, and it is not education.

It is, as with politics, *imposition*.

Imposition of needs.
Imposition of interests.
Imposition of value.
Imposition of mindset.

All to the ultimate effect of nullifying who *I* am, to empty us of ourselves.

Filling us all instead, with *them*.

But, you might object, it is not practical or realistic to have a person-centered education, catering personally to each individual's instincts and character. With the sheer number of children and adolescents that we have in the school system, you may say the traditional, current method of passive absorption is the best that we can hope for as a society, that indeed, better *this* than nothing at all.

Or perhaps, you may admit that this sobering assessment of school is more or less correct but that industry, far from an inhibitor to its reform, must, on the contrary, be the driver, since the most productive workforces require cooperation, open communication, negotiation, and a plethora of other soft and hard skills, aspects that school systems could and indeed should focus on developing. According to this view, the school system needs to remember and revert back to its foremost objective, that is, to provide industry with an able—though manageable—workforce. Hence it might be said the necessary reform is to model the school system's methods and environments even closer to that of industry and for schools to reflect the day-to-day realities and desired qualities of the modern workplace.

This argument may have some utility, were it not for the fact that a school system as such would still be centered on the needs of industry rather than on the persons themselves. Though it might better prepare students for life in industry and may even better engage a child's instincts to absorb and express (even if only to encourage initiative in the workplace), it would still fail to educate in the truest sense of the word and to encourage the full realization of human capability. But proponents of a modern-industry-centric view as such and those of true education can still perhaps find some limited degree of common ground in that school systems are in need of a radical transformation, even if for differing ends and motives.

> And yet, the inertia. Or even movements to the opposite. Why?

If developing a more personalized, relevant, and expressive school environment is insurmountable primarily due to the practicalities of managing a large number of students, then we could build more schools, train more teachers, and provide more incentives and prestige to what is so often a neglected and downtrodden profession. But pessimism as such likely emanates not from material and logistical challenges but rather from a *systemic* resistance to shifting the gravitational center of schooling to the child. Indeed, in many countries and societies, we see efforts made to make school *more* passive, *more* isolating, and *more* competitive; such efforts begin to make sense, almost to the point that they would seem obvious, once we understand that school is a system itself, a fundamental pillar of the wider system that is not for the child and does not care for the child but operates, like politics, to impose an outside agenda designed entirely to serve *them*.

If a large number of children and adolescents is the primary reason for the inability of school systems to practice a true education, then it must be asked why all states and governments of countries where this problem is apparent see population decline and the decreasing number of children as a key societal challenge. With fewer children being born and entering the school system, perhaps the silver lining could be an increase in the quality of education? But the problem with a shrinking population of children is not seen as the diminishment of collective creativity and diversity that results. Rather, states and governments mourn such demographic shifts because fewer children equate to fewer students put through school and thus fewer workers, taxpayers, and soldiers—essentially, fewer slaves. And herein we see why citizens of countries are encouraged and incentivized to reproduce, for children are seen not as human beings each with a unique character and destiny to fulfill but rather as units to carry out the bidding of others, of the system, of *them*.

Indeed, within this system, children are viewed not as people but as workers—mere batteries—to power, operate, and perpetuate the machine that is the system.

In this world, children are born to be slaves.

Still, it could be asked why our current malaise persists if it were the case that, as according to the argument of industry-driven reform, businesses, corporations, and economies would benefit from a more *human* school system, one capable of churning out more job-ready potential employees. Perhaps industry, caught up in its daily business, has not been vocal enough in asserting its needs to the schooling authorities. Or perhaps because industries that require the modern, collaborative, communicative, all-action employee are still very much the minority, and the majority still relies on passive drones doing as they are told.

Or maybe—just a thought—the school system still has a purpose under its current model that goes beyond the needs of industry or even those of states and governments?

Maybe the material cost to industry, states, and governments is in fact a price worth paying?

Maybe the school system, in its pacifying, molding, conforming, atomizing, isolating, and imprisoning of the human mind, and separating us from one another, is doing exactly as it's intended to do?

Just a thought, but a curious one.

We have noted that the people, in the context of politics, seem unable to make a certain choice, that is, to reject an existence of bondage and to choose personal emancipation—to take back power unto themselves—and that this inability stems from not being taught to do so at school. How would the school system as such play a part in inducing this malaise?

Passivity, subordination, isolation, selfishness—these are traits induced by the school system, and it may indeed suffice on these grounds alone to explain why the people do not, and cannot, choose to live unto themselves, liberated and unconstrained by that which seeks their subjugation and indifference. But in addition to this already nefarious list of unholies, perhaps there is one more ingredient that we should add, indeed, one that serves the most to weaken and undermine the mind and spirit.

Ignorance.

Of what? you might ask. Certainly, the school system does not fall short in teaching facts and figures; of this, there is an abundance, an overkill even, to the extent that all but a fraction of what is learned in school is forgotten as soon as the test is over.

No—instead, the school system, by the force-feeding of mostly irrelevant information utterly disconnected and unrelated to the life of the child and through stifling environments designed to suppress individuality through expression, keeps us ignorant *of self*. It provides us with nothing in the way of tools or encouragement to draw out and become the person that is within, that is, to become *ourselves*.

The school system is thus guilty of keeping us ignorant of— blind to—the truth.

What truth?

Of who we truly are and that the power to actualize this person lies within.

Within you, within me, within us all.

The power to discover your identity.

The power to take responsibility for that identity.

The power to represent yourself, to make real the person that you are.

The power to make the choice.

Of freedom over enslavement.

Life over death.

I over *them*.

But again, maybe that's the point? Maybe the school system is intended to hide *me* from myself—to kill *me*?

And by the death—the murder—of *me*, school will compel us to live for something other than ourselves, a cause that is not for the betterment of *us*.

To live instead, in bondage to *them*.

And thereby become engrafted to the system, to become *them*.

Indeed, this is what we see, in all its misery, when we graduate from school and start doing what school was preparing us for all along.

Suited up and ready to go, it's time to get a job!

Chapter 10
Work, i.e. "Jobs"

To talk about our jobs and the reality of how we feel about them is fraught with difficulties and tricky balances. Perhaps this is because a person's job is so often what defines them as a person. It is the source of their livelihood and in many instances that of their families. For a vast number of people, it is also what they dedicate the majority of their lives doing. Thus what people do in their jobs dominate who or, indeed, what, they primarily perceive themselves to be.

In the regular course of life—what we have come to assume as a "standard" path of existence—there is around five years of early childhood prior to formal schooling, ten to fifteen years of school followed by up to fifty years in which we are "at work," hired by businesses to perform certain tasks or perhaps become self-employed and give ourselves things to do. Either way, because our jobs consume such a high proportion of our time, and are the biggest and longest "episode" of our lives, the job we do will often speak loudest as to what we have made of our lifetimes and what contribution (or lack thereof) our lives had towards something greater than ourselves.

In this regard, talk of a person's job and what they do for work may strike a raw nerve. Indeed, since you who are reading these words right now may very well be in some sort of work yourself, with your job tied inextricably to your identity, there is a very real chance things could get personal here. To tread on as few landmines as possible, therefore, I would like to again frame this topic around a single question: Is your job, and what you do for work, an expression of who you are?

It is asking in the truest sense of the meaning—who you *really* are.

Who you were born to be. How you *need* to be, if you are to be truly *you*.

But before proceeding, it is important that we distinguish what is meant by "work" and a "job." The former, as I would define it, is a very general term simply denoting activity with the goal of an end product, effort made to achieve an objective, whether financial, educational, artistic, physical, or intellectual. Work in this sense is apparent in everything that we do as an investment, for the sake of some result. "Job," on the other hand, means something quite more specific. A job is more or less understood as an assignment, that is, a role that needs to be played, a function to be performed, a task to be executed primarily at the behest of something other than oneself.

Certainly, it is entirely possible to "work" for our "job" in this respect, but as with education and school, it is often the case that we conflate the two, whereby "to work" means to get a job and that work takes place within the context of a job. But *should* this be the way that we understand work? Should our understanding of work simply be the carrying out of a request or a command, as something innately reactive? Or should we be aspiring to work for a higher cause, namely, to actualize "who I am," to realize our dreams rather than to satisfy the priorities of an external agent? Even if simply as an aspiration, it is an ideal, I suspect, that most of us feel to be true in our innermost depths.

Thus returning to the question at hand: Is your job and what you do for work an expression of who you are?

Did you choose based on knowledge of self and an awareness of your true identity? Indeed, in choosing what to do with yourself, did you even consider your *self*?

Or was the choice made in a state of darkness, of blindness and ignorance? Or worse perhaps, out of desperation; out of hunger and need?

Or maybe somewhere in between an enlightened awareness and blind ignorance, the best option available at the time?

Considering the central place that work and our jobs occupy in our lives, it is a question of immense gravity and crucial importance. More than any other, the answer to this question, once we reach the twilight of our lifetimes, will determine whether we chose to actually *live* as ourselves.

Yet despite the significance of the question as such—and indeed, our ability to answer as much as possible in the affirmative—the odds are stacked against us, well before we reach the stage to face it. For as we have discussed, the one thing that is imposed upon us, literally by law, as a means to prepare ourselves for work (or rather, to get a job) actively conspires against our discovering and expressing ourselves and the power to thereupon make choices in accordance with who we are. That, of course, is school. And it would be impossible, unjust even, to speak about our choices pertaining to work and our jobs without acknowledging the context in which they are made.

Most schooling systems, as we have seen, are thoroughly depersonalized and mechanistic, focusing almost exclusively on absorbing information about the world outside of the person, whilst disregarding or even actively suppressing the inner world of each individual. Certainly, some of us may attain a sense of our own identity, with a holistic—as opposed to merely academic—awareness of personal strengths, weaknesses, dreams, and ambitions. But as discussed, such instances, by and large, will have been despite the school system and not because of it, for the simple reason that it is not the purpose or intention of the school system to help "draw out" the person within the individual.

Thus in too many cases, upon graduating or leaving school we are for the most part in the dark as to who it is we are, what we are good at, and what we want to accomplish in the limited time we have. In other words, we have very little, if any, idea of the sort of *world* we want to create for ourselves or even realize that we should care to ask and discover the answer in the first place.

Thus faced with the choice of what to do with our lives, we are all too often in a state of blindness and ignorance. And it is in such circumstances of blind intent that we make our choices.

The less we know about ourselves, the less we are able to defend against the bland linearity of life that is expected of us, the presumption that we glide seamlessly from school to a job before retiring and returning to dust. It is perhaps to state the obvious, but without knowledge of self, our *self* is utterly absent at any given stage of this process, for we have no means, no opportunity, to shape and create the process in our image. Indeed, it is in ignorance of ourselves that we live and work not as an expression of *who* we are, but rather according to the prescription of *what* we are as a stipulated identity. We satisfy the criteria of our given function, as specified by authority. We allow our assigned roles and functions to determine our identity and bestow value upon us accordingly. In a very real sense, our jobs *become* who we are. Thus, it is in ignorance of ourselves that we will live regarded as a unit, a *thing*, but disregarded as a person. Without any inkling of who we truly are, the best years of our lives will simply pass us by without us ever having truly *lived*.

But here, a familiar question will pose itself: Maybe that's the point?

If the school system conspires to hide *you* from yourself, to impose a mindset that compels you always to meet the demands of something other than yourself, then to have you determine your identity as one who works for those demands and to perceive your value merely by the ability to meet those demands—maybe that's the intention?

That you are put in a position to make life-defining choices whilst in a state of ignorance about who you are, to thereby live simply as a functioning unit and eventually become solely your *what* in place of your *who*, to think only within a limited and controlled bandwidth when a whole world, an entire universe, lies outside and beyond these boundaries—maybe that's the aim? For insofar that you do not know who you are and thereby what you want, you are powerless to make choices based on awareness as such and liable to instead choose and live based on something else.

Based on what?

Something. Anything.

It does not matter.

What does matter is that your choice is not based on *you*.

It is not meant to be an expression of your identity or make tangible the world within you. So long as you are not choosing and living as *you*, you are doing so as somebody else, for something else—for the country, the economy, the state, the government, the company, the ideology, the religion, the family, the dog, the fame and the fortune—it goes on. For something, anything, except *you*. And indeed, you will do so believing you've conducted your due diligence and made an informed choice to the best of your abilities, having weighed up pros, cons, and viable alternatives. Hence you will stand by your decision, certain it was a free, uncoerced, autonomous decision on your part.

I made the choice, so it must be as an expression of *me*, right?

This must be what *I* want, right?

Right?

But that—maybe—is exactly what you're supposed to believe.

Oblivious that the circumstances were rigged to begin with, that the mindset under which the choice was made was already corrupted, we will believe that our choice was entirely our own doing. Certainly, it was a free choice, in that it involved our own volition, but it was freedom with a key exception—the exception of *you*. And thus at a crossroads and faced with a decision on what to do with our lives, we will make a totally free and sovereign choice to *not* be ourselves. Over and over again we will choose, under the perception of freedom, the illusion of choice, to dedicate ourselves and our lives to something—anything—other than *I*.

We will choose to live and work, through our jobs, for *them*.

And indeed, among those of us living our lives, conducting our daily business, minding our posts, and doing our jobs under circumstances as such, there is a curious dichotomy that has been established between "work" and "life" that is expressed in the clichéd mantra "work-life balance." Now, this might simply be an innocuous phrase to describe the division of one's time—we can't do the shopping, be with the kids, go to the theater, or invest in our hobbies while we're at work!—but perhaps it also reveals a tacit understanding that there is a part of our lives that does not belong to us, that we are not in control of. That indeed, there are things we *have* to do, that are an obligation and duty, contrasted against things we *want* to do. That within our lives there is a divide—conflict—between our will and their control, between freedom and enslavement.

To label one as "work" and the other as "life" denotes that

collectively we see life taking place outside of work and our jobs, that in no uncertain terms, work is nonlife and even negates life. It is a mode of being that, as we have seen, is derived from the school environment, where the natural inclination to express oneself and commune with those around us—our *self*, our *life*—is relegated to the playground and after school, and time in lesson, that is, time "at work," is under the command and supervision of a taskmaster. We develop a mindset whereby work is inherently opposed to the self, that work is not the arena in which we express ourselves and build our world, but rather that of someone or something else. Our understanding of work and our productivity becomes inevitably tied to and justified by the demands of an outside authority—fulfilling a job is the only form of work—while self-expressive activities are treated as unimportant or, at best, assumed to be unproductive.

That being said, however, it is nonetheless the case that "work-life balance" implies precisely that—an existence that attempts to achieve as much as possible a healthy allocation of time to our "life" as well as our jobs. Perhaps in this sense, it would be more accurate to state that we live with a sort of partial freedom, a simultaneous coexistence of freedom and slavery, whereby we may not be entirely owned by our jobs but just rented for a certain period before we are released back to ourselves.

Before settling for an attitude of "better that than no freedom at all," however, perhaps it should be asked which of these aspects, freedom or slavery, most often takes precedence. For it is most commonly the case that our obligations and responsibilities—our jobs—are put above our interests and forms of self-expression—our lives—on grounds that, to say again, we *have* to do the former, and merely *want* to do the latter, and apart from exceptional instances of our employer's mercy and grace or our own courage, "have to" trumps "want to." Such an attitude is considered a cornerstone of being a responsible adult and is lauded by society accordingly. For all intents and purposes, therefore, the slavery within us dominates freedom. Our freedom and self-expression—our *self*—are left to revolve around the gravitational center of our lives, which is our job. Partial freedom is in this respect a pale semblance of actual freedom, the "work-life balance" tipped invariably in favor of work, which we perceive as anti-life. "Free time" is thus merely *borrowed* time, a token donated to us before our jobs pull us back in, rest and recreation before we are summoned once more to the battlefront.

It is freedom at the discretion of *them*—indeed, just as it is in school.

But of course, prioritizing and fulfilling our jobs is not a choice we make primarily for the praise of society or those we work for. It is, more than anything, a choice we must make in order to make money, put a roof over our heads and food on our tables—it is for survival. We are compelled to prioritize that which is paying us, for without the money we cannot even physically live, let alone be free.

Certainly, if money is the only objective, there are a myriad of ways to make money, even using money itself to do so. What a tragedy it is, then, that despite this fact, vast swathes of humanity are consigned to a life of wage slavery, with seemingly no other available means to make money but to sell themselves and their freedom. Indeed, when you cannot produce something as an expression of your creativity and utilize this as a means to a living, the only commodities you have available are your time and obedience, to learn and use whatever skills required to follow orders and execute the tasks put before you.

Here too the fingerprints of the school system can be found. With the incessant focus on feeding large quantities of irrelevant facts and figures, students are left utterly bereft of knowledge that might help them to produce things of value according to their interests, talents, and strengths. This in combination with the refusal to teach anything pertaining to financial literacy, leaves us in circumstances where not only is our perception of money skewed into something that is always paid *to* us, but neither do we have the means—or even the idea—to eventually grant ourselves financial emancipation from the chains of our wage masters.

In this world, therefore, money is for too many people an inhibitor and restrictor to their freedom, a leash that allows them to walk only within determined bounds and never past the lines imposed. To stray beyond, we believe, would spell certain demise, a life sentence condemning us to an existence of meagerness, hardship, and struggle. Freedom, it seems, is the price to pay for our worldly sustenance, and thus with seemingly no other choice, we willingly surrender our freedom and our lives to our jobs and that which pays us. We conflate work with enslavement and enslavement with survival; there is no life without a job, no survival outside of the system.

We are trapped.

Thus we choose to imprison ourselves and surrender our being to bondage. To give our lives to the system, even fight to defend it, believing it is the system to which we owe our lives.

We become the system; we become *them*.

Yet, though it is we who choose our lives as such, going about our daily business, we sense something is not quite right. We hear a murmuring in our depth, telling us something is amiss. Having surrendered our freedom and living a life that is in contradiction with our innermost yearnings and nature—with *who we are*—we notice a certain heaviness, a sadness, a humming anxiety gnawing at our conscience. It is indeed those familiar feelings—

Dissatisfaction. Incompletion. Frustration. Unrest.

Despite everything seemingly okay—I had my breakfast, I've sat at my desk on time, my coffee tastes good, my boss isn't mad—and all being as we have come to expect, we must admit to a certain misery deep within ourselves. And though we can't explain what it is, it is there. We know it; we *feel* it. As an attempt to address this feeling, we might even pick up a new hobby, go on a holiday, buy some expensive clothing, dine at a fancy restaurant, maybe even begin yoga classes, or read a new book—all of course, within our allotted "free time." Failing to find an answer and, indeed, with no *time* to delve deeper—to search *wider*—for what might alleviate this burden of misery and take away our pain, we decide that everything is, in fact, as it should be. Nothing is wrong.

Thus we shift our perspective and strategy; instead of trying to address this feeling, this misery—rather than asking *why*—we choose instead to simply live with the feelings. We learn to accept them, to ignore them. *Life is good. I have everything I need. There are people in worse positions than I am. I can't complain.* So we tell ourselves, but trying to drown out the feelings does not make them go away. Eventually, therefore, we move instead to numb ourselves to the pain. *Drink this. Smoke that. Take this and that. Work harder. Work faster. Get that promotion. Get that money. Get that power.* All our efforts now focused not on finding an answer—on discovering ourselves—but instead, on running away. On blinding ourselves to our malaise, on detaching ourselves from the person feeling the misery.

On *killing* ourselves.

Suicide.

—

Yet collectively our attempts to address this feeling seem to manifest in a rather different form. Though on an individual level we may attempt to run and hide from our pain and powerlessness, as a society it appears we have turned to embrace the one thing which perhaps serves to most constrict our freedom and our ability to live as ourselves: money. On the surface, it seems to make sense, for if we are all working to stay afloat financially, then the more money one has, the more readily one is able finally to pay off the ransom and tip the work-life balance in favor of the latter. Indeed, on these grounds we have invented a culture that glorifies the pursuit and accumulation of money as the way to happiness; we live in a world where, paradoxically, money and the drive to make more of it takes precedence even over happiness itself, based on the idea that we must be happy in our pursuit of money, for money *is* happiness.

And for those of us working in jobs, the same story will be told but with a slight nuance—that we should be happy in pursuing money *on behalf of our company*, for the company's money will cascade down to us as our money, and the more money the company makes, so do we. Thus money is portrayed to us as the way to be *alive*, the path to life, the answer to our ills. It will save us from our pain, redeem and justify the misery we feel inside. In a very real sense, money has become our religion; it has become our god.

But of course, not all among us will fall victim to this false religion of materialism and greed. Indeed, many pity those who are caught up in its crushing wheel. Nonetheless, we are all in search of meaning, purpose, and peace; if not the religion of money, many will turn instead to the *real* religions and worship the *real* gods, to serve something higher, cleaner, and holier as the true way to a better life on earth and joy in the next.

Or at least, what we're told is the way.

Chapter 11
Religion

It is easy to be disparaging of religion and the religious nowadays.

Caught up in their superstition, basing their lives on something so irrational, so unproductive as their gods, spirit, and scripture, in spite of all the enlightened logic and material development that the ways of science and industry have revealed. Clearly, we say, the religious must be stupid, incapable of comprehending their reality through reason and thus resorting to mere belief. Oh, and they must be weak, unable to shed what is probably a religion imposed upon them and choosing conformity over independence. But also frightened, terrified by the prospect of their mortality and thus adhering to fantasies as an attempt to placate their fear. And most pitiful of all, they're probably poor! Having no means to a decent life in the here and now, they must cling to their gods to save themselves for an imaginary—but better—afterlife.

Stupid, weak, frightened, and probably poor—yes, these are

the common traits of the sheep-like religious, so we say.

Yet seen from the perspective of the religious, perhaps the existence of a materialist rationalist, dedicating their life to the pursuit of material gain and worshipping at the altar of reason, is not exactly appealing either. They may indeed seem stupid or, rather, ignorant, not seeing anything beyond the physical and relying solely on intellect to determine what is true and real. They are weak, unable to uphold tradition and instead be swept by the fashion of atheist arrogance. And clearly, it is they who live in fear, too afraid to assert themselves in the face of worldly pressures and responsibilities, unable to live based on what is truly meaningful. And most pitiful of all, they are poor in spirit, filling their hollow existence with mountains of material possessions and the false security that this is all there is to life.

Ignorant, weak, afraid, and empty—from the perspective of the religious, the self-righteous rationalist may come across as such.

And indeed, there might be much to say about this hypothetical perspective from a religious standpoint with regards to modern, "rational" sensibilities. Compared with the religion of money, in which everything and everyone is judged by their price tag, bank balance, and money-making prowess, traditional religion in its variety of forms can often provide solace to those unwilling to judge themselves accordingly. Religion is their connection to something *deeper* and *higher*, a way in which they, others, and the world are afforded value and meaning beyond their material wealth and the ability to monetarily enrich oneself or another. Indeed, religion has its appeal in offering something jobs, school, and the worship of money do not and will not, for they are not intended to—that is, a way to better become *themselves*. It is in their religious environments that people feel they have a framework of guidance and support and, perhaps most importantly, space simply to *be*, without the pressure to produce on demand, to chase the next paycheck and item of desire while listening to the ticking of the taskmaster's stopwatch.

With respect to our relationships also, religion offers a way to commune with more humanity, not merely based on functionality and utility for personal gain but on shared beliefs and mutual support. Whereas school, our jobs, and the pursuit of money induce a certain (often malign) selfishness to advance oneself at the cost of others, religion is able to stimulate morality to live for something greater than just oneself, to offer oneself to charity and the well-being of others, to endeavor to enact positive change within one's means and abilities. And as is commonly misunderstood, the truly religious will act in such a way not because their god or sacred text has commanded them to with the threat of punishment but simply because their religion has inspired that willingness within themselves.

Our modern world so often seems to be all-hands-on-deck to the end of attaining worldly power, status, and possession. And in a society that has succumbed to superficiality, leaving so many of us hollow and bereft in terms of what it truly means to be human—to be *ourselves*—it would seem the greatest power of religion lies not in the guarantee of answers to the most urgent questions of existence but rather in its ability to foster a sense of trust and belief—of *faith*—that a person's searching is not in vain, to provide encouragement during the times of doubt, a light and warmth in the midst of darkness, a promise of salvation and redemption if one can overcome. In this regard, one factor in its undying appeal and longevity through the ages is perhaps its ability to assist in the search, the yearning, for meaning and purpose and to alleviate the misery, pain, and emptiness caused by the lack thereof. And it has shown this capacity not only for individuals but also to foster a desire for people to help one another in their respective quests of searching.

The goodness of religion in the above sense is what we could say is religion at its most *human*. More than anything, it is a depiction of religion as something that cares, that seeks to nurture the psychological, *spiritual* welfare of people individually and collectively, to provide them with support and assurance during times of need and struggle. And what exactly might be "spiritual welfare"? I would argue, very simply, that it is the degree to which we feel able to be ourselves in the most real and truest sense, to simply *be*, without the pressure or coercion to be anything or anyone but the truth of oneself. And I would further argue that the search for meaning and purpose we all at some point experience in our lives is inherently tied to our spiritual welfare and well-being as such, that ultimately, we yearn to become our real and authentic selves, with the level of satisfaction we derive from our lives dependent on the extent to which we are able to be as such and thereupon serve a higher cause through the expression of our respective uniqueness. Thus the search for meaning and purpose implies the process of self-discovery, of finding out the answer to who and indeed what am *I*, and of unraveling one's destiny thereupon.

Thus religion and the fostering of spiritual welfare, in tandem with a true education as has been described previously, are perhaps the two necessary keys to unlock the full extent of human potential. Certainly, the implementation of education in the truest regard could by itself go great lengths in creating unprecedented innovation and progress in a tangible sense. But without the partnership of a person-centered, humane religion, it is doubtful whether people will ever attain *fulfillment* among all the outward advancement. For it must be understood that education is in essence the process of bringing forth the person within and, most importantly, providing the individual with the tools and knowledge to actualize their inner world. Religion, on the other hand, provides the individual with the space to become who they are, the security that it's permitted and safe—that it's okay—to be this person, and to help fight against any temptations and lies that would lead the person astray from this quest for themselves. It is with education and religion in their truest, most human, and most humane forms in partnership and unison that we realize the most complete expression of collective innovation and talent unto the world without but also peace and joy for our world within.

Thus coming to know the crucial importance of religion and education in a mutual, reciprocal partnership for the attainment of what might be the closest thing to collective human perfection, what a fallacy and tragedy it is revealed to be then, that in our current world, religion and education, and most notably the scientific disciplines, are locked and consumed in strenuous efforts to disassociate from one another and even to extinguish one another from the human mind. Clearly, in recent times the offensive is being taken more conspicuously by materialist science and technology to drive out religion and anything perceived as unscientific. Yet in the not-so-distant past, it was religion—or to be specific, politicized and institutionalized religion—that attempted through hellfire and brimstone to eradicate the threat of science or any other such heresy that contravened the official dogma. Though thankfully the age of being imprisoned, tortured, or murdered based on a variance of belief has passed (for the most part), the vestiges of a violent and intolerant religion as such are still apparent in what is commonly perceived as religion today.

Indeed, when people in our day and age claim to dislike and reject religion, it is usually the case they are not referring to the good, humane form—not *that* religion!—but the sort that is committed to violence towards threatening unbelievers, certainly, and that which is preoccupied with ritual, repetition of texts, dogma, indoctrination, exploitation, and condemnation. Namely, a religion that has lost touch with its humanity and a foremost concern for spiritual welfare, displacing the person from the center of its attention, and devising myriad conditions, attachments, criteria, and pressure, that push people to *do* and *think* as instructed rather than simply *be*. Or further, a religion that has sought to aggrandize itself by becoming institutionalized, claiming political power by establishing itself as a worldly authority, and abusing claims of truth to the end of material enrichment. In essence, therefore, a religion—or a distorted misrepresentation of it— that has become about everything *but* the person, seeking only to dominate the individual for its own ends under the guise of a god and providence, to have us identify with and become the religion at the expense of ourselves and our true nature.

Certainly, as we have witnessed especially during the last two centuries, this form of malicious, institutionalized religion has—rightly—been largely beaten back by the rod of evidence and an appeal to the faculties of reason and logic as opposed to mere belief. Yet, as much as the stranglehold of institutional religion on the human mind has weakened and its influence waned in recent times, the insistence on evidence and reason has so far fallen short of erasing religion entirely, and the latter remains as a prominent and important aspect of societies globally. One possible reason for this has already been discussed—there appears to be a desire within us for something deeper, a way to better become *ourselves,* something that material science and other such avenues seem unable to provide. So long as this desire persists, it is likely will religion also, and while it is hoped religion is becoming more humane and person-centered, the search for meaning and purpose—the yearning for oneself—is still very much liable to be manipulated for ends in total opposition to oneself by religion in its more sinister forms.

Indeed, a religion that dismisses the person and instead promotes an excessive, even exclusive, fixation on ritual, text, rules, dogma, and the like will by definition serve to undermine rather than support any quest for self-discovery. And this for the same reason that "education" in school does not educate in the truest regard: rather than helping people *become* who they are, focusing solely on obeying commandments and living within defined boundaries will very quickly cause them to lose sight of their identity and may eventually see their character and confidence die entirely. To be sure, religion does not have to be institutionalized for it to be stultifying in the above sense, and it is often present not only in environments purposed for religion but also in the home. How heartbreaking it is to realize, then, that the victims of such malicious and damaging types of religion are so often young children with the least means to intellectual or emotional self-defense and that it is imposed upon them by their parents, relatives, or guardians, whose foremost role it is to ensure their nurture and well-being.

Yet while the above may be the case, it is still religion in its organized, politicized, and institutionalized form that best showcases its tendencies to operate as a *system*, that is, deliberately arranged in a certain manner so as to produce a certain outcome. For although religion practiced by domineering and dogmatic people in homes or elsewhere is incredibly harmful to spiritual welfare, it is not systematic to the extent that there is an element of randomness to its occurrence—one case is not exactly related to another and likely caused by the perpetrators simply not knowing any better, perhaps due to themselves having been victims in a similar sense. In grassroots examples of such instances, therefore, there is certainly damage and indeed *death*, in the sense that it is suffocating of individuality and the ability to *live* as oneself. But in the case of malevolent, institutionalized religion, this becomes the actual intention. Either by deliberately turning a blind eye to suffering and evil to protect its material trappings and influence or by intentionally killing the mind and spirit of a person in order to subjugate and enslave, such a religion will serve only itself on the altar of whatever god it pretends to venerate.

There is a famous adage that power tends to corrupt, and this is perhaps especially so in relation to political power. Once a religion has been established as a worldly, secular authority—or even while it is in pursuit of such status—either through joining forces with existing political structures or forming its own, it must necessarily vest upon itself a certain disposition that is conducive primarily to the attainment and expansion of power. As a result of this politicization, which can only be described as a process of disfigurement, a religion motivated by power will naturally prioritize the amassing of material wealth and influence over spiritual nurturing and the morality that underpins this. For indeed, it arguably would not seek to establish and impose itself as a worldly authority to begin with if it were concerned first and foremost with the spiritual development and well-being of its adherents, which, to be sure, has no correlation to the material or political grandiosity of a religion. Yet what is most insidious and deceitful of such religions is that they will use the mask, the pretense of spiritual nurturing to the end of what is their actual priority, with all manner of fiction and falsehoods invented as means to these ends.

Perhaps the most fundamental aspect we see among these types of malicious religions is the presence of a hierarchy of some form, that is, a chain of command in which religious authority is ranked and structured. One might rightly argue that hierarchies are apparent in all forms of religion, including the "good" sort of it. Yet there is a crucial difference when there is an understanding that the foremost role of the leadership is to let *be*—to exercise knowledge and wisdom in aid of a person's quest of self-discovery, providing the space and support for an individual to become who it is they are through the encouragement to confront and accept the truth of themselves. When a relationship as such is formed for and at the level of the individual, then at once any sense of a hierarchy, with all expectation of conformity and compliance is removed.

But whether it consists of just a single charismatic leader or a complex and multitudinous web of levels, ranks, and positions, almost invariably the first commandment of a power-centric religion will be obedience to the structure—do and believe as you are told, for the ones put above you are the ones with knowledge of god, and it is solely through them and their teachings that you will come to know god (and attain blessings, go to heaven, etc.). In a similar fashion to politics, therefore, whereby the power of a given representative or party is justified by the popular support of people, such a religion will justify the authority of its hierarchy on grounds that it represents the will and truth of god on our earthly plane and is acting as its closest intermediary.

As we thus become beholden to the whims of a despotic religious hierarchy, the individual is degraded to perhaps the most wretched, fearful, and lamentable form of mental and spiritual slavery. We are led to believe that the institution and leadership of the religion must be treated as if it were a god, and based on the self-proclamation that it is the representative of their god on earth, in very real terms, such religions will convince its believers that following deception is in fact following the truth, with spiritual growth thereby becoming synonymous with complete adherence to the orders, teachings, and modes of thought prescribed by the religion itself. To do, say, and think as the hierarchy instructs literally becomes a divine command, with guilt and punishment for an inability to comply, or worse, actual death for those unwilling.

It is based on this megalomaniacal doctrine of divine representation that tyrannical religions reveal their most intolerant and brutal underbelly, with repeated and prolonged episodes of genocidal murder taking place throughout history by religions that label all who disagree and dissent with it as an enemy of their god, deserving of torture and death. Yet while the murderous tendencies of such religions may seem somewhat removed from our everyday reality (though it is not by any means merely a thing of the past), we are still very much able to perceive the divisive effects on those who follow religions derived from this mold. Though it may no longer be common that slanderous labels such as "heathen," "heretic," or "infidel" are branded against another directly, a misguided sense of superiority and "otherness" is often exhibited by believers who, having absorbed the prideful self-righteousness demonstrated by their particular religion, display similar tendencies towards those they consider morally or spiritually inferior.

In addition to the above, however, we can recognize further malign and corrupting influences on human interaction. For whereas "good" religion in its more humane form will inspire the desire to perform kind acts of selflessness, charity, and positive change among people—an instinct which lies within us all as naturally social and cooperative creatures—a malicious religion bent on power and control will abuse and manipulate this same desire so that people will direct their goodwill not to others and their own spiritual development but to itself. It will exploit what is perhaps the purest, most high, and most joyful instinct of humankind, the desire to do good to others and develop oneself, and conflate it totally with its greed. Service to others becomes servitude to the hierarchy, and the development of self becomes absolute obedience to its words and instructions. And there is no prospect of a return for such bondage, though the religious leaders may provide hollow assurances that "something" will come, supposedly in the form of blessings or good fortune, either in this life or the next. But apart from such empty promises, these pernicious religions will proceed to take, take, and take some more, leeching off their adherents to fatten themselves whilst preaching the virtues of unconditional giving to justify it.

Now, upon absorbing all of this, you may wonder aghast how anyone can believe, let alone act upon, any shred of this crap from religion. Clearly, you might say, the victims of exploitative religions must be stupid and only have themselves to blame. But before snatching at the trigger with the gun of judgment, let us take a moment to consider: when you have no sense of who you are (school), no satisfaction in what you do since it is not expressive of who you are (jobs), no means to tangible self-expression based on who you are (school again), and disillusionment with people, groups, and structures wielding power on your behalf to make decisions that only seem to worsen your circumstances (politics), then the prospect of finding deeper purpose and meaning—finding yourself—in something or someone that claims to offer exactly that probably can seem incredibly alluring, even irresistible. Indeed, it can be doubly difficult when predatory religions offer tidbits of truth and crumbs of what we truly yearn for, exciting our hopes and compelling discipleship.

For religion as we see it today is perhaps a mixture of the "good" type with the evil and malice of systemic, power-driven religion. Certainly, it is entirely possible, common even, to find communities and environments of nurturing, giving, charity, and warmth within the framework of the latter. Indeed, with the dawn of the age of reason and the often absurd doctrines of corrupt religions coming under more scrutiny than ever, the institutions and hierarchies simply would not survive to the degree that they do without the presence of such communities—and it is precisely upon the backs of the good-hearted people among their flocks that these religions justify themselves. Using the environments of kindness that their adherents create as evidence of the good intentions and virtue of the organization and hierarchy, malevolent and harmful systems of religion will cite them in their defense as excuses to escape change, reform, or abolishment altogether.

Therefore, it must always be remembered that instances of goodness within the context of destructive and toxic religious institutions are invariably exceptions, taking place despite the nature of the religion and certainly not because of it. For as with all pillars and aspects of the wider system explored thus far, the point and purpose of these systems of religion are never *you*—only *them*.

Chapter 12
In Conclusion

Thus concludes our brief tour.

Four key pillars—politics, school, work, i.e. "jobs," religion—though undoubtedly there are many more subsections and cross-columns that might have been added. All are created, manipulated, and imposed upon us as *the system*, to arrange our world in such a way to imprison the human mind within boundaries defined by *them*, to constrict freedom and choice to options conducive only to *them*; to have us choose, think, work, and pray to serve only *them*.

To kill *us* and enslave us to *them*.

What drives the system as such? Why does it move so obsessively, so compulsively, so categorically to impose ignorance, to stamp out *me*, to so powerfully undermine the person and the means to its self-expression, both individually and collectively?

What does the system want?

Even based on our limited exploration, it is clear there is one defining aspect of the system as such. We can distill the system into one word that is the common denominator, the single motive that ties together all pillars of the system, coursing through its veins like its lifeblood, sustaining and spurring it forward towards its ultimate end.

Control.

It seeks to control you, control me, control us. Thus the system opposes life and that which makes us truly alive. It seeks to kill and destroy us, not physically (though it perhaps might if it is threatened enough), but above all psychologically and spiritually, to destroy what makes us unique, what might allow us to express that uniqueness, what unites us, and what would allow us to be free—our *spirit*. And thereby it seeks to enslave us, for us to become vassals, mere batteries, to power not ourselves and our destiny as unique individuals, but only the system—*them*.

All this for no other purpose than control. By debilitating our minds and eliminating even the idea to become ourselves, the system will have us live our lives only for *them*. As we have seen, all aspects of it are driven fundamentally to crush us and to keep us in darkness. Aided by the ignorance that it induces, the system robs us of the opportunity to cooperate with one another in building *our* world, in accordance with who we are. The system has instead created a society—a prison—in which we do not own our lives, and where we are moved inexorably to make choices and live in bondage to *them*.

The conclusion, then, is clear: the foremost aim and intention of the system is to create a world and society favorable only to *them*, to elevate a particular class over everyone else, and that the system seeks to enslave us for this purpose.

Certainly, it is self-evident that specific groups of people outwardly benefit more from the system than others. Further, there is little doubt that the system is a *human* creation, configured by those with power to keep the masses powerless and thereby maintain the master-slave hierarchy that is so forcefully imposed by the system's machinery. Thus it would seem to make sense—the system is built by the masters, for the masters, with each of us molded and manipulated by it to serve as their slaves. The system exists to push their agenda, to empty us of ourselves and fill us instead with *them*.

To have us become not ourselves, but *them*.

The ominous *them*; this was referring to these self-serving masters all along.

This much is palpable and perhaps unsurprising. But if we determine that a particular group or class of people impose themselves upon the rest of humanity through the system, then it must be asked why we, the victims, so easily surrender to their advances. Why do we seem so incapable of standing up for ourselves? Since there are no chains or physical restraints to our choices or actions—since we are free—why do we not act to emancipate ourselves from this wretched state of mental slavery?

Some reasons for this have already been put forward—the system's duping of populations into believing they are free with merely the perception of choice, as well as rigging and corrupting the mindset in which they make choices—but maybe, looking deeper, we can identify another, more underlying factor.

Fear.

It is fear—fear of another, fear of uncertainty, fear of strife—that maintains the system as necessary within our collective minds. We fear that, without it, order will collapse into chaos, our livelihoods will run dry, our neighbors will turn on us, and terror will reign free. Conflating the system with survival and stability, we justify the system and our place within it, convinced it is a necessary force to protect and preserve the people. Indeed, the system has itself played on this fear, stoking the flames of anxiety and suspicion to embed itself within our consciousness as the guardian of security. And as it paints the picture of an increasingly dangerous and bleak world, it has come to demand more and more of our freedom in the name of protecting our freedom and safety—ultimately, with us even surrendering *ourselves* in exchange for our preservation.

But this fear, even in conjunction with the system's trickery and hoodwinking, does not fully explain our utter defenselessness against the devious ways of the system. If we are being gradually swindled out of our freedom, our mystifying inability to resist and to simply swallow whole the terms of a social contract being continuously changed to our disadvantage is telling of a deeper malaise. It is as if we have no grounding or means whatsoever to defend ourselves, with no sense of the things yielded to the system in its unremitting quest to further its control—namely, our freedom, our lives, and our identities upon which we direct our freedom and shape our lives. And our overwhelming passivity as the system continues its march forward to domination, trampling on everything that makes us *who we are* along the way, reveals to us what is the root of all our ills.

Ignorance.

Not merely of our predicament as slaves, or of *self* owing to the system's force-feeding and saturating of our minds. Beneath and beyond these aspects, it seems we are afflicted with an ignorance more pervasive and fundamental, one that is inherent to our human nature and that underpins all other forms of ignorance that are inflicted on us by the system.

We are ignorant of God.

Of God we are ignorant, and of everything that flows from God to us as imparted truth. Namely, we have lost sight of the *image* of who we truly are; how we are supposed to be, the person we are to become in order to truly be ourselves. We are born under the shadow of this ignorance, blind to the truth and with our spiritual connection to God already severed. Having no recourse to the truth imparted by God, we are without an anchor for our perceptions or guidance and direction for our choices. Thus we are rendered rudderless, akin to an aimless herd of sheep ripe for exploitation by wolves in shepherds' clothing. We are left weak, exposed, and bereft; defenseless and incapable of resisting the forces of deception and manipulation that lead us away from ourselves for selfish gain. And though we might have the *feeling* that something is wrong and that, somehow, our lives are not how they are supposed to be, with an absence of clarity as to *why* these feelings abound we will proceed to kill them—kill ourselves—and be led astray, our psychological suicide leading to bondage and our bondage leading to the creation of a world only for *them*.

This affliction of inborn ignorance and inherent disconnection from God, I suggest, is what many have referred to as *original sin*. From birth, we are in darkness and in exile, removed from the source of all true meaning and identity—God—and from *life* in accordance with the truth. We are, in a very real sense, born under the curse of death, already blind to and "missing the mark"[8] of how we are meant to be—the only person we can ever be and the only life we can ever live if we are to be truly *alive*—that is, as ourselves.

It is my belief that we are all under the yoke of this original sin. All of us, whether master or slave within the system's structure, are lost and blind. We are all in ignorance, we are all missing the mark, thus we are all living as something or someone other than our true selves. No one is who they truly are and, to say again, whilst we are afflicted by this fundamental ignorance we are all liable to be ensnared by deceptions that fill the void of truth in our minds, causing us to pursue and, ultimately, *become* untruth.

It might seem anathema to suggest that even the masters of the system are, in a sense, victims. After all, as the creators, inheritors, drivers, and beneficiaries of the system, are they not the deceivers of this world? Is it not *them* who manipulate, imprison, and enslave, extinguishing even the possibility for us to discover and live as ourselves so that we exist solely to serve *them*?

---

[8] In the Hebrew Old Testament, the word that is translated into English as "sin" is *khata*, and in the Greek New Testament the word used in the same context and likewise translated as "sin" is *hamartia* (noun) or *hamartano* (verb). Both the Hebrew and Greek words are broadly defined as "to miss the mark."

True as this may be, the absolute ubiquitousness of original sin points to the reality that the masters, being human like the rest of us, have also been deceived upon their inborn ignorance. Indeed, I have come to conclude that even the system itself, with all its insidious trickery and mind-crushing machinery, is in fact a product of ignorance and subsequent deception. Being shrouded in darkness and oblivious to their identities like us all, the masters have succumbed to the lure of power, wealth, and control. They have elevated these as their idols and prime motivators to be worshipped and attained even at the expense of others, to the extent that they would impose this entire system of slavery and death upon us all.

But if the system is not the *source* of deception, what then, is? If, rather, the system is a product of ignorance and deception, who or what does the deceiving? Or is it simply the case that human beings, born ignorant and being innately fallible and willful, are naturally predisposed to pursuing self-interests at whatever cost? The answer, I suspect, is a combination of the two; that is, human beings are innately ignorant, fallible, and willful, but there is also an active, *non-human* force of malevolence that works ceaselessly to deceive and destroy us.

In this world, there is some *thing*, some *one* that hates us—something indescribable, something unspeakable, something terrible. It is a manifestation of pure evil, totally dedicated to negating life and opposing the truth. It is a force that actively intends for us to remain in ignorance and separated from God, sowing deception in our minds to have us live in pursuit of something—anything—other than the truth of ourselves, thereby keeping us yoked to original sin and under the curse of death. And just as God is the source of all meaning and truth, I believe this force, this being, is the origin of deception and untruth.

It is the Devil.

As the prime deceiver of this world, it is the Devil who has led the masters of our world astray. Exploiting their ignorance and extraordinary willfulness, it is through *them* that the Devil has instigated the construction of the system that imprisons and enslaves us. Thus, in very real terms, the Devil has manipulated humankind for us to deceive and kill one another. It is through the system that the Devil infiltrates and infects our minds, the system serving as the Devil's conduit to fill our minds with falsehoods. Led astray by the Devil via the system we are denied the opportunity to attain *life* in the truest sense, but being ever ignorant and oblivious to our folly, we—master and slave alike—will continue to partake in this system and, by our own choice, proceed to give our lives to causes that serve only to exacerbate our predicament of ignorance and death.

And it is important to note that, although the system may be geared to realize a society that is conducive solely to *them*, in the eyes of the Devil the system is but a means to our collective destruction. Thus there is no particular allegiance or favor on part of the Devil towards the masters who seek to profit from the system. So long as humanity remains trapped in deception, preoccupied with chasing what it *thinks* is real and important, it does not matter to the Devil who benefits, what sort of world we create, or where humanity ends up, for any world or place that is not in accordance with the truth is, by definition, an untruth. It is a lie, a missing of the mark—it is a *sin*—born from falsehood and disconnected from God.

It is clear, then, that the Devil moves to deprive us of truth through continuous deception so that we fester in exile, alienated from the truth of our being and from God, for posterity. And, indeed, for us to perpetuate our state of exile *through our own choices*. But having gone some way towards understanding the Devil's malign influence, it is perhaps natural to wonder: What is the Devil's objective? Is there even one? Or is the Devil content to simply witness humanity become ensnared by its manipulation and fall headlong to destruction? To deceive and destroy us, I suspect, is an integral aim, but only insofar that this serves to accomplish the Devil's ultimate intention: usurpation.

Earlier it was stated that, in our state of inborn ignorance, we are all susceptible to deception causing us to pursue and, ultimately, *become* untruth. This end of us becoming something—anything—that is not the truth of who we are, I believe, is what the Devil most seeks. With our minds already clouded and blind to God's imparted truth from birth, the Devil, through the agency of the system, supplants the *image* of who we truly are with lies and deceptions. Saturating our minds with everything and anything that we are *not*, the Devil causes us to misplace our identity in falsehood and to persist in lies—for us, eventually, to *become* a lie.

The Devil usurps God's imparted truth as the focus and aim of our lives, thus we become living manifestations of the Devil's usurpation.

Living our lives together under the false direction of the Devil's deceptions, we create a *world of sin* reflective of our state of untruth.

We remain yoked to original sin and become not the truth of ourselves, but the Devil's deceptions.

The Devil usurps God; the Devil becomes our god and we *become* the Devil.

And, indeed, it is the system that turns us into the Devil.

It is through the system that the Devil transmits its hatred and spreads its lies. The system is, in very real terms, the corporeal substantiation of the Devil on this earth. The system is thus not merely one of control—it is also a system of deceit and hatred. As does the Devil, the system deceives us; the system *hates* us.

The system poisons the minds of all who partake in it, that is, of both master and slave. The system compels us all to discard our identities and to become what *it* requires us to be; there is no room for you, me, or us, other than as cogs and gears in the machine. The system depends upon our continued ignorance of who we truly are to survive. It *hates* the truth, thus it will do everything in its power to hide and kill it to ensure we live to maintain the system's advancement. And the system will secure itself not only through means of psychological assault to eradicate any inkling or desire within us to seek the truth, but as well by luring us into its stranglehold through the promise of everything that we hunger for as human beings: belonging, identity, purpose, recognition, approval, security.

It is up to us, however, to realize that the system can never fully satisfy our deepest, innermost yearning as unique individuals, namely to simply be as ourselves and to find acceptance and belonging as ourselves. This, by definition, can only come about as a result of us seeking and becoming the truth of who we are and creating a world centered on this endeavor. Insofar that any such satisfaction is derived from the system, it is requisite on us vesting upon ourselves an identity that is not *I*—on us becoming who we are *not*—in order to fulfill a role, a function, a task that is demanded of us. To become, as mentioned, a cog in the machine. But as all parts in a machine are disposable and replaceable, so too are we if we cannot or will not execute our vested duties.

Thus the system's promise of belonging, identity, and purpose is entirely illusory; it is fleeting, conditional, provisory, contingent. In this respect, any sense of security afforded by the system is in fact *insecurity,* and any recognition or approval is based on its *disapproval* and *rejection* of who we truly are. Nothing is truly real or absolute in the system except the requirement to kill oneself and tie one's being to bondage.

At this point, it is perhaps appropriate to ask the question again: Why do we not break free from the system's hold? Why, despite all its malevolence and the suffering that it inflicts upon us, do we cling to its skirt as a hapless child? With regards to the masters of the system who are its primary beneficiaries, the incentives to keep the engines running are perhaps more conspicuous in terms of the worldly power, wealth, status, and control that they stand to attain. But what of the rest of us, for whom there is comparatively very little such temptation or pressure to remain within the confines of the system? Certainly, numerous formidable factors that inhibit us from making choices to the end of self-emancipation have already been discussed. But even after coming to realize the depth of our predicament and, indeed, the freedom and power that we have to overcome our malaise, how many will answer the call to actually do so?

Do we even *want* to be free?

The answer, I suspect, is that the majority of us do not, to the extent that any exhortation to choose *life* in the truest sense is ignored or condemned. Stained with original sin and born into the system as its children, we have become all but dependent on its pillars upholding all areas of our existence, organizing our lives, feeding us with choices, promoting idols and gods to worship, telling us what to think. Thus, in addition to the variety of fears that have been inculcated into our minds by the system, perhaps the greatest fear that we have come to possess is simply the fear of ourselves.

We are terrified of the prospect of our own freedom and the potential that we might live unto the truth, simply as ourselves. Consumed by our fear and weakness, we choose to be cradled in the arms of the system, unable to bear the thought of stepping out of its shadow. We dismiss out of hand the idea that we might exist without it; we argue in its defense and ostracize those who merely raise the suggestion of its abolishment. The system has so infiltrated the modern mind that we have exiled ourselves even from our own imagination and the possibility that we—together—could not merely survive but indeed create a better world. But alas, it is by an inability to entertain the thought that we crawl unto the system on our knees, akin to a helpless and dependent baby looking only up, unable and refusing to see ourselves and each other.

Thus we choose to remain in the system, and thus we choose to remain in bondage.

> Over freedom, we choose enslavement.
> Over life, we choose death.
> Over *I*, we choose *them*.

We choose the Devil.

Alienated, distant, and fearful of our true selves, it is by our own choice that we remain in captivity, in exile—in *Babylon*.

And yet, though it is we who choose our lives as such, we cannot escape the dissatisfaction, the incompletion, the frustration, and unrest felt towards our predicament of self-nullifying psychological slavery. With each passing day that we live in this state of surrender and servitude, there grows a sense of hatred, of *resentment*, first towards the system as the perceived source of our malaise but increasingly towards ourselves as we subconsciously recognize our own culpability. There is perhaps room to maintain that we are but victims in all this—having been kept in darkness and deceived by the system since the very beginning, are we not simply living the consequences of the system's intent? Yet, it is to our collective discomfort that despite all such reasonings and excuses, the truth of freedom remains, and it is in our weakness that we assign blame and in fear that we fail to muster change in our lives. As the outward hostility towards the system turns inward towards ourselves, therefore, we eventually come to hate not only ourselves but also others we might perceive as more free, and who thereby serve as a reminder of our inability to exercise power to express our own individuality.

The hated thus become the hateful, and thereupon we see the emergence of a creature driven and consumed by resentment, by hatred. Crippled and defeated by the system, we eventually become the system—we become *them*.

> We become evil; we become hatred.
> We become the Devil.

Yet, some may still ask why all the doom and gloom. *Life isn't so bad! What have you got to complain about? There's so much good all around—you even said it yourself! Stop being so negative.* Some might say. Or somewhat specific to politics: *Sure, the system has problems, but it's brought untold benefits to so many! Who or what will build all the roads and hospitals, and maintain our vital infrastructure?*

On the latter, if only it was the case that the system in the form of states, governments, and representatives dedicated itself solely to delivering on public infrastructure and services, so as to create better and healthier environments for nations to live. It is evident, however, that states and governments are concerned with so much more than mere infrastructure—indeed, their primary concern is always *politics*, that is, the expansion and consolidation of power for themselves and their sponsors (primarily the latter perhaps), with the achievement of aims independent from and often opposed to the people. Infrastructure in the name of politics as such is perhaps a tool states and governments employ, but rarely, if ever, is it delivered purely as a means for the public good.

Yet it is a clear sign of our collective malaise that we cannot seem to separate politics in the name of power and vital infrastructure needed to go about our lives. Indeed, states and governments throughout the ages have cleverly conflated the two, leading us to believe everything will stop and fall to pieces without their active intervention and for us to reject the prospect of the system's absence based on this fear. But who's to say we, the people, cannot deliver on maintaining and improving our living environments without state or government mediation? Indeed, who is it that actually builds the infrastructure and provides the services? And even if a level of bureaucracy were required for funding and organization, where is the need for politics in the name of power? The consideration of such questions is vital if we are to start the process of filtration between the system and our collective needs.

Statements that appeal to the seeming reality of a more or less good life under the system, I would argue, are also driven by a similar misconception. That is, the notion that the system "gives" people freedom and rights, whether freedom of speech, freedom of association, right to education (despite the problems with school), universal suffrage (despite the shortcomings of representative democracy), and so on, out of benevolence, progress, and, well, because the system just isn't *that* bad. To be sure, even a rudimentary knowledge of history would reveal that freedoms and rights as such were not by any means "given" to people; they were obtained and won *by* people, in most cases only after prolonged and often bloody episodes of struggle and activism by the enslaved, oppressed, and downtrodden against the particular incarnation of the system during their period. Therefore, to suggest that the freedoms we are blessed with were granted to us by virtue of the system would be a colossal insult to those who fought to win these freedoms. In the same vein, to state that the system today is more or less sound and does *not* conspire against us would be manifestly wrong.

But there is what we might call "the problem of good" still outstanding, the contention that if the system is as evil as claimed and its entire machinery is so irresistibly geared towards our downfall—indeed, with the added burden of inborn ignorance in the form of original sin to boot—shouldn't there be only evil in our world or at least a lot more of it? Why is there any good when we should all just be mired in hatred, corruption, selfishness, and indifference, with no concern for ourselves or others?

One line of reasoning could be that, despite the system's deeply malign influences, there is still a natural propensity within us to commune with and aid one another, due to the evolutionary advantages such positive patterns of behavior have offered our species throughout the ages. Or to offer a more spiritual perspective, that the presence of original sin has not divorced us from God irreversibly and though we may not *see* truth with any clarity, we have retained our capacity to at least *feel* some semblance of right and wrong in accordance with it.

In this regard, perhaps it cannot be said that the system's hold on our minds is total and complete just yet. We still possess a fundamental essence of what it means to be human and despite our deep-seated, multifaceted ignorance that is innate, imposed, and self-perpetuated, we still retain an instinctive memory and impulse to aspire for higher states of being both individually and collectively. But other than broad-stroke speculations as such, I can only wonder. Truly, what a marvel it is that we find countless examples of altruism, empathy, forgiveness, growth, learning, creativity, cooperation, and mutual understanding—of *humanity*— within the system at all, in defiance of its relentless drive to divide and subjugate us. If nothing else it is a miracle in itself and, even more, a testament to the vitality of the human spirit.

Yet, as was discussed previously, those who defend the system will often cite such examples of goodness to justify the current state of it, to exonerate the system from condemnation and argue that, at its core, it is humane. Such naivety, however, is rooted in a similar mindset that entertains the aforementioned notion of a "good" system "giving" freedoms and rights to the people. It need not be repeated that the acts of virtue that we see all around us occur despite the system and the unequivocal hatred and megalomania that drives its hand. The conflation thus of the goodness that we see despite the system and the system itself must stop. In order for us to fight, to be free, and to become ourselves—to realize our destiny and all that we *could* be—it is imperative that we see the everyday acts of goodness and virtue as the miracles they are and the system for what it truly is: a machine of hatred—of enslavement and spiritual desolation.

Wake up!

Part 3

Band Together

Unity. Resolution.

Chapter 13
When Am I? How Am I?

Do you have a dream?

A picture of how you would like to be, but more than that, an intuitive sense of all that you *could* be? What I am referring to is perhaps related to *those* feelings that have been central to everything thus far, but I will refrain from mentioning them again by name. For as much as they are real and have been instrumental in telling us that something is wrong—with the world, and within ourselves—it would be a mistake to become fixated on them and excessively interrogate ourselves for answers. This would lead to stagnation as opposed to learning and growth and, in this sense, while we attempt to free ourselves from the system's psychological captivity we must be wary to not imprison our own minds in blame and self-doubt.

But in the context of our analysis of the system, and now that we perhaps have gone some distance in identifying the incredibly powerful and malevolent structures that intend and cause us to be in darkness, there will, I'm sure, be a very strong tendency for the feelings of dissatisfaction and searching to mutate into anger and hatred, or even despair. Indeed, you may very well have been feeling such emotions already, even before you laid eyes unto these words.

The system, as we have seen, is a machine of evil and hatred, seeking at all costs to destroy us and any possibility that we might live as ourselves. It would be natural for us to shy away in fear or to want to return the sentiment in kind, that is, to hate the system with all our being, to dedicate ourselves to its destruction and wipe out any chance for its reappearance in any shape or form.

Hate that which hates you. Destroy what seeks to destroy you. Kill or be killed.

These, to be sure, are our instincts; basic, natural impulses that emerge in us without any conscious thought or deliberation. Indeed, it is instincts as such that have allowed our survival through the ages. When we are threatened—by danger, by a predator, by an enemy—our reaction is to fight and destroy, to neutralize the threat in order to stay alive. And here we have most definitely identified our enemy, perhaps our greatest nemesis, one that seeks nothing but our death and enslavement. If there were any circumstances in which our hate was justified, surely it is now? If there were anything that deserves our hate, something that *must* be destroyed by any means, surely it is the system?

To feel this way, and maybe even proceed to act upon this urge, would be natural.

But is that what we are? Indeed, is that all that we *could* be?

It was in asking myself this question that I was reminded, totally unexpectedly, of the story of Jesus Christ. I was not by any means living a Christian life or engaging with relevant literature at the time, and despite some fleeting interactions with the Christian message many years prior, neither did I have any habit of referring to Jesus' life and teachings for inspiration or guidance. It was, therefore, rather odd that out of all the things that could have popped into my mind, I suddenly remembered Christ in thinking about how one ought to respond to the system's malign and destructive influence. But as it turned out, by following this trail that had serendipitously appeared before me, it soon became clear that everything I needed and more was found in Christ.

There is much that can be debated on the topic of Jesus' life—miraculous birth, healer, teacher, performer of miracles, leader of twelve disciples, ultimately betrayed by one and sentenced tragically to death by crucifixion, to rise again three days later to give hope and inspire missionary zeal—and its meaning, certainly if we consider the many alternate insights that have surfaced challenging the traditional narrative.[9] While I would not want to dismiss any of this as insignificant or as nonsense (as many in our day tend to), for the sake of relevance I would like to focus on one particular aspect, that of his betrayal, torture, and finally death by crucifixion. For it is in the episode of Christ's

---

[9] See for instance, the various Gnostic texts that have surfaced as part of the Nag Hammadi library or recent critical scholarship of the New Testament by figures such as Bart Ehrman. While such discoveries and works have offered challenges, however, there appears to be a strong consensus that the fundamentals of Jesus' story as presented in the Bible is reliable (see for instance the works of N.T. Wright, Gary Habermas, and Richard Bauckham, among others).

crucifixion and the immediate events leading up to it that we find, in the purest and clearest form, an example of overcoming the instinct to hate and destroy, or to simply fall into despair. Christ shows us what it means to rise above our natural impulses as such and to become and attain something higher.

Following capture by the authorities of his time, and a sentence to a brutal death despite his complete innocence as a result of a sham trial, upon the cross Christ perhaps had every reason to resent, hate, and hold spite against all those who—while mocking, beating, and insulting him—drove him to a miserable, painful death. On the other hand, having been betrayed and deserted by his disciples and forsaken even by God,[10] it could be said he had equal reason to abandon all hope and spend his last moments in silent despondency.

Yet faced with it all, Christ chose strength in the truest sense of the word; strength that reveals itself in acceptance. He maintained his dignity, faith, and graciousness, choosing to utter the words, "Father, forgive them, for they know not what they do"[11] and commit himself to his Father God upon drawing his last breath. It was there, upon the cross, that Christ chose to love humanity and God when tempted, in the most irresistible fashion, to hate and to fall into the darkness of despair. And by his choice as such, Christ defeated all temptations and the unspeakable treachery which sentenced him, triumphing in the name of good and righteousness with the cross, once an instrument of torture and intimidation, transfigured to a symbol of hope and shining glory. The story of Christ's resurrection thereafter is a confirmation that he (literally) rose above to live again in peace and joy, free from

---

[10] Matthew 27:46

[11] Luke 23:34

any shackles or residues of hate and negativity.

It is easy to think of this story as completely "other" to ourselves. That it happened to a person called Jesus, in and around the land of Israel some millennia ago, at the hands of jealous, intolerant, and oppressive forces. Tragic, yes, but in the distant past, and thus irrelevant to us today. However, even when the moral message noted above and the contemporary significance is elucidated, it remains easy to perceive it through the lens of "Jesus did that," implying that we are exempt from holding ourselves to the standard and behavior illustrated, especially considering Jesus was the Son of God, the Messiah, and we merely fallible mortals.

But I would like to suggest that the story is real. Yes, in the sense that it happened to Jesus all those years ago, but also, that it is happening right now, all around us, and it is happening to you, to me, to us. The system, the machine of hate, captures and imprisons our minds to deny us the means to live according to our true identity, in order to enslave us and impel the building of a world only for *them*. Every day that we live in this state of bondage, we are not living, but dying, for we are living not as ourselves but as something, anything, but ourselves—as *them*.

As the Devil.

Born ignorant by the curse of original sin and with the system's ways imposed on us from birth, psychologically we are dying insofar that we are unaware of our true identity and have no sense or wherewithal to actualize ourselves. Further, we are dying spiritually, cut off and alienated from God who is the source of all truth, meaning, and *life*. And an existence that is ignorant of truth and separated from God, inhabiting a world begotten by these shortcomings, is indeed tantamount to bodily, physical death. Through the manipulation of our mindset and choices, the system compounds our inherent state of "missing the mark," that is, of sin, of which the inevitable consequence is separation from God and thus death.[12] In a very real sense, we are driven and condemned to our deaths—tortured and crucified by the hand of the system—every single day.

Indeed, Jesus himself underwent a similar ordeal on the cross, pronouncing, *"Eli, Eli, lama sabachthani?"* that is, "My God, my God, why have you forsaken me?"[13] as his tortured body hung to die. According to Christian teaching, Jesus was not speaking in parables or metaphors with these words but was in fact crying out in direct response to the breaking of his communion with the Father, which was a necessary ramification of him taking on our iniquities and having become sin on our behalf.[14]

The story of the crucifixion, then, did not just happen to a man called Jesus all those years ago. It is happening now, with us as Christ.

We *are* Christ.

Upon this spiritual and psychological crucifixion that we experience every day, we are powerfully tempted, as Christ surely was, to hate that which hates us and sentences us to death in the

---

[12] Isaiah 59:2 states, "Your iniquities have been barriers between you and your God, and your sins have hidden his face from you so that he does not hear." Thus the Biblical understanding of sin is anything that causes separation between God and humankind. As elucidated in previous chapters, it is my position that a separation from God is coterminous with ignorance of truth, and that truth is the only basis upon which we can attain life in the realest sense.

[13] Matthew 27:46

[14] This particular interpretation is eloquently explained by Derek Prince in his sermon *Jesus Tasted Death In All Its Phases*, a part of his *Spiritual Conflict* series of lectures.

most unjust and insidious of ways, or to despair in the face of what seems an insurmountable enemy. Christ, however, chose to have faith, forgive, and love; he rose above all temptations and our sins that were imputed to him and was resurrected to show he had conquered and overcome everything—even *death itself*—to live again in power and glory.

Thus we must ask ourselves: Do I have the strength to make the same choice of forgiveness and hopefulness to be reconstituted in new life beyond death, just as Jesus was?

If we are to release ourselves from the grip of the system and, upon our newfound emancipation, begin to live so as to build *our* world, then it is a choice we must make; the temptation has to be resisted. For if we do not, then the hatred or despair will consume us and we will be left as nothing but shells of anger or victimhood, possessed by the craving to destroy or crushed by hopelessness that makes us lie down and be destroyed. If we go the way of despair, nothing of our predicament will change and we will simply remain a casualty of the system's malevolence. Should we go the way of anger and hatred, we may break the chains of bondage tying us to the system but only to be enslaved again, this time by our own bitterness and animosity. And whether the system or our hatred, it does not matter; so long as we are enslaved, the Devil wins. Evil has the last laugh—and entirely at our expense.

Therefore, through the precedent set by Christ and by engrafting ourselves to his indomitable spirit of love, we must rise above through strength and forgiveness. Indeed, knowing that we are all—master and slave alike—ignorant and deceived, but forgiven by the mercy of Christ for our part in the world's chaos and discord. Only by the choice to forgive and overcome upon being forgiven can the indignation or despair we may very rightfully feel be transformed into a desire for reconciliation and the creation of a new and better world. It is imperative that we follow in the footsteps of Christ, that is, to face our tribulation with the same grace and fortitude that he embodied to break the cycle of hatred, despair, and destruction, and find redemption from the shackles of enslavement.

It is in Christ that we find all we need to overcome this test of the heart, and through him that we are enabled to take back everything that has been yielded to the system. Upon our hearts and minds being set free from any resentment or anguish, we can finally begin to imagine and build a new world—*our world*—upon the remnants of the old.

But of course, the practical questions: When does this happen? *How* does this happen?

All these things—finding ourselves, fighting the system, rising above hatred and despair by emulating Christ, and creating a new world for us—just seem so *big*. Surely, it can't be little *me* who must do all this?

Well, actually, yes. It is you. It's also me; it's all of us, together. And indeed, we already know how. All it takes is a choice and it is a choice we can make right now, at this very moment. Why don't you give it a go? It's easy if you try, and it isn't hard to do. Close your eyes and declare these words however loudly or quietly you wish; it may even be most effective if you meditate and just proclaim them in your heart. However you do it is up to you, but just give it a go.

Ready?

I am who I am.
I am *me*.
I am *I*.
I am.

How was that? *Just words*, some might say. But they are words that, if spoken with intent, contain power. Thus, we must do more than merely *say* these words, we must *declare* them—we must proclaim to the world, to ourselves, that we are no one and nothing else but ourselves. We must shed our old skins, release ourselves from all impositions, of all the chains that tie our being to something other than ourselves. Through the uttering of these words, we enable ourselves to transcend what are simply our experiences as a life form on this earth to become *awareness* of our experiences. We are no longer held captive by the trappings of this world, the designation of ourselves as merely *this* or *that*, and vest ourselves with the power to separate from any limitations set upon us thereby. In the truest sense, we are enabling ourselves to become unlimited—to become infinite.

Through these words, we are setting ourselves free and returning to the essence of our existence.

We are returning to the truth. To *I*.

Considering the gravity of that statement to the topic at hand and, indeed, its centrality to all the ideas, questions, and assertions raised on this journey we've traveled together thus far, let us take a moment to unpack it. It should be clear by now that what allows us to live in a way that is most real and what the system moves so compulsively to inhibit and stamp out is, above all, *knowledge of self*. That is, an awareness of the truth, the *image* of who we truly are as imparted to us by God.

It is only upon discovering and knowing ourselves truly that we can determine what is desired for this self, the tools we require to actualize this self and to defend against anything that acts to deceive us into serving something other than this self. Thus the truth of our identity is our sword and shield, the means of protection against falsehood and the weapon by which we assume sovereignty over our lives to forge a reality in accordance with the truth.

The process of *becoming* this self, however, is slightly more convoluted than the common wisdom of our day would suggest, which is that we can simply choose whoever or whatever it is we want to be or that there is no preordained nature within us beyond our experiences and base instincts as animal creatures. To my mind, the process of becoming ourselves in the truest sense consists of a mixture of choice, creation, and most importantly, acceptance.

Certainly, we have the freedom and power to choose to live either as ourselves or as something else. *That* we choose to become ourselves is up to us, and the world we subsequently create as a result of our choices is our *creation*. Yet the most vital and crucial aspect that so often seems to elude (or be refuted by) our modern conceptions of identity is the *what*. That what—and indeed, *who*—we discover upon exercising our freedom is not a matter of choice. Who we truly are is, in fact, given to us by God as our inheritance. It is rather like life itself—a gift, one we do not choose but rather are chosen to receive. It is simply there, within ourselves, immutable and ever-present. And it is our role as free, autonomous agents endowed with power to uncover this gift within; to seek it, to encounter it, and thereupon to accept it.

I can, and must, choose to become *I*.

To direct my freedom so as to create unity within myself,

unity between who I choose to be and who I truly am as I find myself—unity between I and *I*. Eventually, to realize a state of being in which there is no distinction between the person I choose to be and the person I truly am.

A state in which I simply *am*.

And upon establishing this unity that is complete and absolute, we find a resolution to perhaps the greatest mystery of our lives: *who am I*.

I am who I am.
I am *me*.
I am *I*.
I am.

This attainment of internal unity and the fulfillment of identity is, I believe, the essential mission and purpose for all of us on this earth today; indeed, it is one we can accomplish only for ourselves, for the simple reason that only I am capable of becoming *I*. Every life is thus irreplaceable, and in the same vein, every life lived in ignorance of its true identity and purpose is a loss never to be recovered. Such is the tragedy of the ages that so many—too many—people do not live their lives with an awareness as such and in many cases do not even seek to attain it. For it is no less the uncovering of truth—the *image* of our real selves—the person we are born to be, who we *must* be if we are to be truly alive.

That I am *I* is the truth. It always was and will always be the truth.

It is reality. It is our destiny; the identity in which past, present, and future come together in unity.

And it is upon returning to this truth, that I can now see—

I am simply *I*, as you are simply *you*.
We are no longer tied to labels or separated by borders.
There are no lines that divide, no boundaries.

No limits.

There are no sides and therefore no enemies.
There is only unity.

Unity—a band—between you and me.

Acknowledging that we are thus totally and absolutely free and that our freedom has a purpose, a direction, an aspiration, a destiny, what comes to your mind? What are your dreams? Better pay attention, for it is in our dreams that we picture a better *me* and imagine a better world. Upon the choice to become ourselves and the determination to seek and live only according to who we truly are, the person who was once exiled from the imagination— our true self, *I*—is now front and center.

What does this person want?
What must I do to make this person real?
How do I best express the truth within me?

With a new and invigorated mindset, one that is free from

the system's hold, we can begin to ask and indeed answer these most pertinent of questions to our lives. Perhaps for the first time, we can start to *work* for ourselves and invest in that which builds *our* world. For it is by virtue of the choice to be *me* that we cease to live as *them*. Our minds are released from the Devil's deceptions and we can begin to walk the path of truth in the grace of God. Truly, we are no longer enslaved and can assume the rightful position as masters to our own ships, sailing in the direction as guided by the bestowed truth of *I* and our innermost desires thereupon. Where will your journey take you? What *could* you become? Indeed, the answers will become apparent as we move forward and continue the process of our self-discovery in the crucible of our lives, plumbing ever-greater depths to the uniqueness of our person and the infinite wonders that lie within.

And just imagine, if you and I, us—all of us, together—were to live in such a way. The culture we could express, the nation we could build, the world we could create by the power of our unity. Living without limitations to our being, so will the possibilities be limitless. With the evolution of ourselves, a revolution of the external world will occur naturally and inevitably. As if a mirror revealing only our reflection, the world without will be but an expression of the world we have discovered within. There will be no thunder, no lightning, no mountains crumbling or seas roaring; rather, with every individual awakening, with every shedding of impositions and borders, with every choice to be free, we will inch closer to the world we could have—until one day, the last cog in the machine will simply stop. Politics will evaporate, children will be educated, work will become expressive, and religions will help us *be*. On that glorious day, we will rise and, with the light of the new dawn, open our eyes to find the old empire has quietly collapsed, the system failed, the world created only for *them* vanquished.

In its place, we will have built a new world without limits or confinement; a world of truth, expression, communion, and unity between us all as one whole.

A world where we belong; a world that we have created. Freed from our captivity, we will return to our rightful home. We will return to *Zion*.

And upon our return, looking back at how far we have come and the road we have traveled, we will see—

All it took was a choice.

Part 4

Love

Alpha. Omega.

Chapter 14
God

Does God exist?

In our time, the question is conflated very much with religion, perhaps for the obvious reason that it is religion that traditionally espouses itself with the subject of God and with many claiming to "reveal" or "bring us closer" to God in some manner. But as discussed in our exploration of religion as a pillar of the system, it is often the case that religions as such have used the device of representation to their own ends, presenting their beliefs, commandments, leaders, hierarchies, and institutions as synonymous with God and the sole way to God. However, as we have developed a healthy skepticism towards dogmatic religion through the agency of reason, we have also largely done away with the concept of God along with it.

We, in our time, believe upon the predication of reason and for reason to be a matter of evidence. If we can prove beyond reasonable doubt and be told by evidence whether or not God is a reality, we will believe. In this regard, when we speak of evidence as it pertains to the existence of God, we are, presumably, examining the claims of traditional religions—that an all-powerful God created the universe and all living things within a certain timeframe and sustains all the forces governing the phenomena apparent. Indeed, the burden of proof should be upon the shoulders of the ones making such claims, we say, but the case as compiled by modern, rational humans would suggest that reason, or rather science, does more than an adequate job of explaining the universe and its functions without reference to God. Thus the conclusion that science essentially "explains away" any need for God—though it may not actively disprove God's existence, it has made the intellectual requirement for God's existence, especially in the sense of a creator, defunct.

We live in a world where any such "search for God" is conducted primarily through observation of the physical universe and the accumulation of ever greater amounts of information as evidence, upon which we deliberate and judge. This, to be sure, is symptomatic of our modern, collective psychological and spiritual predisposition. We assume that everything is to be found in the world outside of us—identity, authority, options for choice, education, work, knowledge, evidence, rules, health, well-being, morality, meaning, purpose, ourselves, the truth, God—all to be found, or rather, provided, from somewhere, someone, or something other than ourselves. Our role, it would seem, is merely to behold, interpret, and explain within the boundaries set; essentially, just to react and to obey what is external to us.

Hence why in our time there seems to be so much interest in and emphasis placed on the opinions of scientists and other such experts, who possess the ability to tell us what is going on based on their deep knowledge and understanding of all that is outside of us, that is, the world of physical phenomena as determined by observable, quantifiable, and verifiable features that can be perceived and presented as evidence. We predicate that the world external to ourselves is a shared reality common to all. If something "outside of us" were to happen, then we can all observe it for ourselves, or at least we have recourse to the outside world for evidence and verification, and thereupon to use our capacity for argumentation to convince others to see and agree on how it is to be perceived.

It is this sense of the universality of the outside, physical world that has convinced us of its paramount importance for society and ourselves. The truth as it pertains to us all is "out there" in a form external to us, and our collective stance is one that hungers for and demands information of this external reality so that we might make well-informed choices. Indeed, would it not be foolish—suicidal even—to ignore the environment in which we are situated? Should a creature of the wild not be equipped with an awareness of surrounding traps and dangers, it would be destined only for the jaws of a savage, predatory beast. If it manages to stay alive by virtue of its wits, however, the opportunity is opened to perpetuate the species and may eventually even see its kind come to dominate the environment, to shape and exploit it to serve its needs, thus further ensuring survival and progress.

Likewise, it is for us in human society—we are driven to explore and understand the world outside of us first for survival, so that we might react in accordance to the state of the world as we perceive it. If it is a bad, threatening world, with perils and enemies all around, then we can take appropriate measures to self-defense by activating our suspicion and moving to subdue or annihilate a cause of danger. This is perhaps not far off the mark in terms of how humankind has hitherto sought for its security, that is, by taking control of the world externally, suppressing, pacifying, or enslaving anything it feels threatened by—including and especially other human beings. Though certainly not the exclusive factor in their progress, science and technology have themselves been propelled and incentivized greatly by this will to dominate, their fruits to be applied to neutralizing an enemy and command of the earthly environment thereby. But whether for such destructive motives or otherwise, comprehension and a harnessing of the external world is without a doubt *the* primary preoccupation of our species in this age.

In our time, truly we have come to be fixated on the world without. Information on it is our most precious commodity, for the power that it grants the knower and the advantage that is guaranteed by this power. Indeed, beyond our mere survival and safety, knowledge of the outside world is the wind that guides our sail to the final frontier of human existence: a state of omniscience and thereupon the ability to exert absolute control upon everything external to us. Through complete knowledge of the external world, we become the most effective, most efficient, most potent, and most correct; it is, no less, our means to perfection.

It is the way by which we become gods.

It would seem somewhat ironic, then, that the majority of us, consumed by the obligations and pursuits brought unto us by the outside world, are thus inhibited from leading an orderly and effective life by the very thing we strive to understand in order to attain it. Amidst our bustling and hectic routines, because of which we have no bandwidth to pursue knowledge for ourselves, we have come to form a dependency on others, that is, our scientists and experts, who have made it their mission to observe that which is "out there," and convey their findings to the rest of us. What they show to us, we take as our evidence; thus the scientists and the experts, specialists in a particular aspect of the external world, are treated as the new truth-bearers of our age—bringers of light illuminating a murky and mysterious world, helping us to see a clearer vision of reality "out there," which we have come to believe is the only reality worth knowing. Through the torch that they shine before us unto the world without, our external field of vision is expanded, and we feel we have a better grasp of what is actually *real*.

Thus with our most capable, worthy, and trusted scientific experts at the spearhead of human civilization and driven forward by the supremacy of the scientific worldview, today we find ourselves in a situation where the most mind-blowing science and the greatest wealth of information within our known history are right at our fingertips. The best minds of our species have voyaged far and wide, examining every accessible facet of our visible universe, from the most gargantuan stars and galaxies to the tiniest, most minute details of subatomic particles. And in the process, the sure ground where God once stood as the mighty creator and sustainer of our mysterious world is rather turning to be an ever-receding fog of scientific ignorance, indeed, with us mortal humans rapidly occupying what was once God's divine jurisdiction. In such circumstances, we perhaps could be forgiven for entertaining a hint of suspicion that God may not in fact be "out there" as we once thought. After all, if evidence for the existence of God were simply a matter of gathering data and explaining what we see, surely it is already there?

But, alas, the findings of centuries of discovery do not seem to have revealed God in any of the nooks and crannies that the peering eyes of science have mulled over. There may be patterns—hints and nudges to suggest "maybe"—but nothing appears to be definitive. Hence, seemingly upon the recommendation of modern scientific expertise, we do not believe.

Or rather, we do not care to believe.

Faced with an ever-increasing volume of information, hypothetically it could very well be that one day, considering everything and tying together the vast depth and variety of knowledge we have accumulated, to advocate for the existence of God suddenly becomes the rational position among the establishments of reason. But presented with a logically bulletproof, eloquent, and intelligible explanation of God—the holy grail of all science—the reaction for the vast majority of us, I can almost guarantee, would be to simply shrug our shoulders, to turn away in apathy saying, "so what?"

For the information, the evidence, the so-called proof is cold. It is distant. It does not care and does not speak to us individually. We will always perceive it as something "out there," that is, something outside and alien to us, and thus never close and never truly real. Any such proof will do nothing to change our circumstances, nothing to provide answers for the deepest, most burning questions relating to our being, nothing to take away our pain. Hence, we will not care for the evidence either, be it for the existence of God or any other holy deity.

God may or may not be dead, but to us, God is as good as dead.

Yet if anything has been clear in our journey together thus far, it is certainly possible that the truth, in the sense that it relates to us *personally*—who we truly are, what this person desires, and our destiny therein—is to be encountered and discovered not from examining and accumulating information on the world without, but from seeking within. If all the evidence the world has to offer has not been satisfactory (and arguably never will it be), then perhaps we could benefit from a shift in perspective, although this would not, in all likelihood, be upon the advice of our scientific truth-bearers, considering it is an area modern science has vacated and even trivialized on the grounds that it is "subjective," unverifiable, and therefore irrelevant to the development of our species.

Indeed, anything pertaining to the inner, spiritual world has been shunned and plastered with a label as "unscientific" (and thus deserving of denigration and condescension) by those assuming the supremacy of science. Looking at our own behavior, however, it seems there is still an innate drive to delve within when seeking solutions and insights into our lives. Even within this overly-scientific era in which we live, it is a curious point of observation that most activities—be it prayer, meditation, or deep personal reflection—that aim to find answers or achieve a certain state of mind in relation to our being, and indeed a higher *consciousness*, naturally incline us to close our eyes. It is as if we instinctively know that answers to our innermost existential questions are to be found not through the use of eyes meant for perceiving the natural world outside of us, but rather that we must search the unseen inner world of *spirit*.

We must close our eyes and *gaze within*.

Therefore, if introspection is an instinctive, naturally occurring form of inquiry, it suggests that the world within ourselves offers another avenue for the finding of answers, an additional reservoir of truth that is *specific to us* and thus beyond the methods and explanations of the scientific method and material evidence.

So, does God exist? Upon the above, it begins to creep up on us that maybe, having had no luck relying solely on examination of the external, physical universe, we might want to try a different approach, that indeed, we may have been looking in the wrong place all along. By entertaining the thought that we can find truth by looking within, we might even dare to ask the question: Could it be that God is found likewise?

Could it be?

And if God is found within ourselves, could it be that God's existence has personal significance for us—in very real terms, that God is in fact a *personal* God?

Could it be?

Indeed, it was suggested previously, that the truth that lies within us is nothing less than the truth of ourselves, that is, who we really are, the *I* within I. Further, it was maintained that this person within us is rather like a gift; we do not choose to have it, nor do we decide who or what it is. Rather, our role as free, autonomous agents is to direct our efforts to seek and discover this person, so that we would become ourselves in the most real sense and assume our true identity. The starting point to this process of *becoming* lies in waking up to the reality of evil and our state of bondage, making the choice to free ourselves from deceptions and impositions to become *awareness* of our experiences, thereupon to be released from all boundaries, delineations, and limitations—to declare that I am no one else but myself. After a period of searching under a renewed mindset and having released ourselves from all lingering resentments and regrets through belief in Christ, we eventually start to see who it is we are and what we truly desire— we encounter the *I* within.

This encounter and the continuous process thereafter of directing our freedom to attain unity between ourselves and our true selves, thus to fully become *I*, is the purpose and mission of our lives. For indeed, it is the only life we can ever live if we are to exist as ourselves, based on the truth. And upon this all-important encounter on which everything—past, present, and future of not only ourselves but of the whole world and entire universe—rests and is based, we will experience the most strange, wonderful, and beautiful phenomena.

We will sense, with no other way to describe it, that this person is loved.

Something loves us; something indescribable, something ineffable, something incredible. It is a love that suddenly puts everything into perspective. All the questioning, the searching, the period of ignorant bliss before the searching, all that has transpired to cause the searching, all that has transpired to lead to answers—all of it, everything, was in order to encounter this truth, this gift, within. To thereupon understand, to *feel*, that we are loved and that even while we were in darkness, we had been loved and carried all along. Everything has fallen into place and is thus at once redeemed. And upon coming to know the truth of *I*, we have the opportunity to live the life that only we can, to become the person we were born to be, to hone our uniqueness as our most prized treasure and contribution, without which the whole world, the entire universe, will not be whole.

Everything—the past, present, and future of ourselves, the whole world, and the entire universe—rests upon this encounter with the truth and knowledge of the love we were cloaked with all along. In our awe, we will find the only word available within our limited vocabulary—indeed, the only word deserving—for such intelligence, serendipity, grace, and benevolence.

God.

Even this, however, may seem inadequate, hence why perhaps some traditions will refer to it as G-d, as a means to honor its sacred mystery and ineffability. But inquiring, challenging, and defiant creatures that we are, we will attempt to describe the indescribable, to place a word on something seemingly so big, so great, so wonderful, so enigmatic yet so personal as God. Racking our brains to muster a term, a phrase, a name, or a concept that will encapsulate everything about our discovery of God, there will be none other than that which we have come to understand God to be.

Love.

God is love.

And there is no other word, no other feeling, that will adequately describe what we have come to experience and know.

Love.

God is love.

This encounter with our true selves—with *I*—is nothing less than an encounter with God, and thereby with love. It is a love that serves as an invitation for us to love ourselves. Knowing that God loves this person, encourages us to become this person, and has so cleverly worked with and through our choices and circumstances for us to encounter this person, we are thus invited in the most irresistible fashion to accept and start becoming our true selves—to begin a new chapter in our lives guided by truth, free from impositions, lies, and deceit. With and by the love of God, everything was set in motion and everything has been redeemed to allow for life anew.

Truly, God is the Alpha, the beginning of everything.

And it is upon the knowledge that we are loved by God that we can stand strong and confident in our being. We shed all fear and attain the power to withstand and overcome any force that has reason to not want us to pursue truth and to be ourselves.

However, it is important to note that although the love of God may guide us to encounter our true selves and thereupon invite and encourage us to become this person, to continually seek and make choices to the end of attaining unity between I and *I* is a matter of infringeable freedom on our part. And make no mistake, the road to attaining that unity—especially in a world that is ruled by this system of hatred and enslavement, conspiring by any means to crush our spirit and keep us in darkness—is hard. It is unimaginably hard, being mired in confusion, doubt, misinformation, manipulation, errors of judgments, distractions, wrong turns, struggles of all forms, and even physical harm and persecution. At times the pain and tribulation may seem unbearable, and we may very much be tempted to cease our searching, to stop thinking, to stop choosing *I*, and instead walk the path of least resistance and deceit, to lose ourselves and slip back into the system—into the arms of evil, the Devil.

But through it all, the love of God sustains us. If we look within, we will find power. We will find strength, and we will find a way. For although the love of God cannot *cause* us to make any choices, it serves, in the most loving and profound way, to provide encouragement in times of weakness and struggle. It offers perspective through the light of revelation during periods of darkness, doubt, and confusion. If we just look within, we will know and feel that we are not alone.

That some *thing*, some *one*—God—cares.

One may indeed ask why this is. Why does God care? Why does God love? By way of an answer, we can remind ourselves of why the system and the Devil hate us—in short, because they wish for us to be destroyed. And upon our destruction and the eradication of truth from our minds, they will have us become slaves to imposed aims and falsehoods to perpetuate our alienation from truth.

The system and the Devil thus seek *death*.

But while the system and the Devil hate us and work to destroy us, God loves and desires nothing more than for us to be our true selves. God will leave no stone unturned for us to be set free from bondage and live completely as ourselves because that is the only way by which we attain *life*. And why does God wish for us to be *alive* in the truest sense? Simply, and merely, for love's sake. God loves us and wishes the best for us for the sake of love, because God *is* love.

God is thus the Alpha, the beginning, and indeed it is God through love who carries us thereafter and throughout. But is there an end? Just where is all this heading, we may rightly ask. The answer, it would appear, is one that we have already encountered.

Unity.

That we fully become who we truly are, as we find within ourselves. That we attain total unity between I and *I*. To realize a state of being in which there is no distinction between the person I choose to be and the person I actually am.

A state in which I simply *am*, to just *be*.

To live life in such a way that expresses completely, in all respects, the truth within us. In very real terms, to *become* truth.

It has been said that the search for meaning and purpose in our lives is synonymous with the yearning to become our true selves and further, that the sense of meaning, purpose, and therefore satisfaction that we derive from our lives is dependent on the extent to which we exist in such a truthful way and serve a cause higher than ourselves thereby—that we contribute to *us* as a whole, through the becoming and expression of *I*.

It is certainly a mysterious phenomenon, whereby we, in the form of the truth within us, desire for ourselves to become this truth for the sake of our fulfillment, and that we experience the love of God in a manner that coaxes us to persevere to this end. It is almost as if our true selves and God share the same aim and that, either by the same will or each possessing a will of their own, desire for us to attain unity with the truth of ourselves within. Which one is it? God and the truth within—are they separate, or are they one? In trying to pin down the answer, a familiar sense makes itself apparent.

Neither definition fits.

The truth of *I* and God are one and the same, yet they are wholly separate. The two are both, and yet they are neither. Multiplicity is the answer. God and *I* are completely one and utterly distinct, both at the same time, and hence they are neither.

God is the truth within, the truth within is God.

The relationship cannot be described, bounded by definitions, or restricted by terminology. It is both, it is neither. It is more. It simply is.

This line of thought, however, leads to a rather astonishing realization—the *I* within myself, my true self, with all its particularity, multiplicity, and radiant individuality, is God. It is an aspect of God, completely and utterly unique only to myself, bestowed to me as my gift. God is my creator, the source of my identity; God has imparted an aspect of God to me, and unity between myself and my true identity—between I and *I*—is in fact unity between myself and God. And by the becoming of this truth, I become the corporeal *image* of God that only I am able to become.

God is thus the infinite wellspring of all true meaning and identity, and it is God from whence the infinite variety of our individual identities are derived. We all share equally in God as distinct and unique image-bearers of God; we have each been gifted a person to become and for us to embody this identity is to embody the particular truth imparted to us by God. The purpose and mission of our lives in this sense is to become fully ourselves and to thereby become, in our own right, fully God.

>I am who I am.
>I am *me.*
>I am *I.*
>I am. . . God?

It is utterly astounding and perplexing to equal degrees, but with all things considered, it begins to dawn on us—incredibly and terrifyingly—that this indeed is the aim. God is the goal, the final and ultimate destination.

God is the Omega.

But faced with this most daunting and seemingly impossible of goals, it is the boundless mercy of Jesus Christ upon the cross that provides us with all necessary wherewithal to rise with the challenge. For any regret or bitterness towards a past life we now know was not lived in truth or to overcome any present predicament of pain, torment, despair, or suffering, the unfailing love of Christ grants us the forgiveness, fortitude, and grace to move forward, step by step, in our purpose to manifest completely our truth within.

But as extraordinarily difficult and distinguished as it most certainly is, perhaps there is more to be gleaned from the story of Christ beyond continuous meekness, humility, acceptance, and resistance to temptations to the end of becoming our true selves. Indeed, Christ taught much else during and through his life, with perhaps the most important message above all being the astonishing claim that he is one with God—indeed, that he *is* God—and that no one comes to God but through him.[15]

How can this be? After all, as great and saintly as Christ undoubtedly was, was he not simply human like the rest of us with an equal stake in the infinity of God? Based on what has been said, it is perhaps feasible that Jesus was someone who had accomplished this mission to fully embody their God-given truth and walked the path of their divinely-ordained destiny to its ultimate end. Therefore, would it not suffice to conclude that Jesus was simply one with God? Surely, something is amiss in asserting that he *is* God.

No matter how outlandish it may come across to our modern mindsets, however, if we take into account everything about Jesus' life, death, and resurrection as well as his various pronouncements claiming divine authority, then to infer precisely

---

[15] There are numerous passages in the New Testament which are used to support Jesus' claims to divinity, but here I am primarily referring to Matthew 11:27 and 16:16-17, and John 8:58, 10:30, and 14:6

this is logical and even necessary. And if it is that each of us are aspects of God and that we derive our true identities from God, the idea that Jesus is God—if accepted—can mean none other than Jesus himself being the same source of all meaning, purpose, and identity that God is.

That, in very real terms, each of our individual identities are sourced in Jesus as they are in God, and that the spirit of Christ dwells within each one of us as does the truth of God.

We are each unique portions of an infinite creator God from whom we derive an identity, a truth, an *image* to become. In Christ the individual, Jesus the man, however, is not simply an aspect of God, but *all* of God. In him, God has poured out the entirety of God's being, and thus the identity of every single facet of the living universe is contained in Christ as it is in God. We are each *an image* of God, temples that are individual hosts and expressions of particular aspects of divinity. Christ, however, is *the image* of God, the one divine temple that houses all others; one individual in which the identities of everyone and all are imbued. And just as God *is* the source of identity and truth for all things in existence today, God *was* the source of identity and truth for all things in the past and *will be* the same for all things in the future. Likewise, the truth of all things past, present, and future are contained in Jesus. In him, all eternity coalesces into a single human being, and through him is the way to God and our true identities.

It is a truly awe-inspiring, mind-boggling thought, but in the mind of Christ, there was no hesitation or doubt, no veil of ignorance or blindness covering knowledge of his identity as such. Christ was born from a woman as a man and was among us as fully human, yet at the same time as fully God. This was Jesus' identity that God had bestowed to him, the truth of who he was, a truth with which Jesus was completely united. Truly, Christ was without sin, with no sense of "missing the mark" or being separate from God in any way. Being in a state of complete unity between himself and the truth of himself, and therefore with God, Jesus was the first truly *human* one who was fully *alive*; the Son of God who came as the model of perfection, a person who so embodied his God-given nature that he himself came as God and all that God is—love.

Christ lived and died as the unblemished, indisputable expression and incarnation of love. Thus he was, is, and will forever be, the perfect and absolute image of God as flesh.

Christ is God.

It is in following the example of Christ, by engrafting ourselves to him and his spirit of unyielding love that we learn to embody the essence of God. It is in walking with Jesus that we are enabled to *become* ourselves, united with our truth as Jesus was his. It is through forgiveness, in love, that we become our true selves and thus become as God, as love. It is in Jesus that we are redeemed and made righteous, shown a path to victory in the face of pain and defeat; it is through Jesus that we are offered a way to be returned to none but our true selves and back thereby to God.

Christ is God and Christ is the way, the truth, and the life; the path unto which we shall be united with the truth of ourselves and with God—for us to become truly *alive*. Our physical existence becomes a corporeal manifestation of unity with God, our bodies transformed from a graveyard under the curse of death to a temple abounding in life-giving truth.

Christ is thus the redeemer, the Savior, bringer of redemption for a wayward humanity groaning in the darkness of bondage and exile. Further, Jesus is Lord, under whose guidance we are returned home to his kingdom—the kingdom of God—where in willing subjection we are granted freedom from death in ignorance and offered everlasting life in truth that is eternal.

As a result of oneness and unity with God through Christ, we can attain what we might say is "totality of being." We become an absolute manifestation of truth, in that we fully embody nothing but the truth of our identity. Thus we are set entirely free, emancipated from all labels, boundaries, definitions, limitations, and impositions. We become unlimited, infinite. Thereby we are totally unique, existing only as *I*, as our own individual incarnation of God. And upon this totality—this wholeness—of being, our lives and the world that we create for ourselves is one that expresses completely the inner world and self we have cultivated. In the most real sense, we begin to live the life that only we can live, become the person that only we can become, the person we were born to be, the only person we must be if we are to be ourselves. Thereupon we bestow unto the world—*us*—our most treasured asset and most precious gift.

I.

Now, it is probably worth pausing here to discuss a point of concern that is likely causing alarm bells to ring hysterically in the minds of many. How can we be sure that one person's truth, and the process of them "becoming God" no less, will not be used to justify acts of heinous treachery, injury, and even murder? Knowing full well the tendency to rationalize or explain away crimes with the excuse that "God said so," what will serve as a restraint to probable, or even inevitable, excess and transgression by an individual or group vying for domination? Without any assurances, deterrence, or mechanisms for protection against potential threats, all this talk of self-realization and "totality of being" may very well seem to be just pie in the sky, a fanciful flight of the imagination with no grounding in the reality of a coldhearted and brutal world.

Certainly, it is a valid concern, one that is rooted in the deep-seated mistrust and fear that we hold towards one another, hardened by generation after generation of unspeakable abuse, injustice, and betrayal. Yet even in the face of what seems to be the harsh fact of our existence as such, it must be remembered that God is love. And if the truth within ourselves, our true nature, is derived from God, then it must follow that our own fundamental essence is also love.

Who we truly are, this person is loved. More, this person *is* love, for this person is an aspect of God, and God is love.

Thus the process of becoming ourselves is by necessity a loving pursuit. Any and all endeavors undertaken to the end of unity between I and *I* must be an act of love, born from the invitation of God's love to love ourselves, and thereupon for us to behave in a manner that is loving towards ourselves and others. By definition, therefore, an action that leads to the injury, deception, or enslavement of another cannot stem from the sincere quest to become the truth of oneself. To the contrary, it must necessarily be rooted in *ignorance* and in the hatred, selfishness, greed, fear, insecurity, and weakness that is born from blindness to the truth of love within ourselves and a willful disregard thereby of the value of another on grounds that they precisely are "an-other," with their suffering thus having no bearing or relation to us. Indeed, it is the system of hatred itself that would put us in such a state of ignorance and spiritual, psychological isolation, a dark hole in which the further we fall and become disconnected from truth, the greater our proclivity for atrocities and monstrous acts of violence, deceit, and destruction.

On this basis, we will come to see that the freedom of each individual to discover and actualize their truth and all necessary support therein, far from being a cause for inevitable strife, is, in fact, the only way to the realization of genuine, universal joy and peace. To attain a world that is only of truth and love, each and every individual must grow to become the truth of themselves and thereby become love; with the world and society we thus create simply a reflection, a natural product of our collective expression as beings of truth and love.

However, even while we undergo the process of this transformation and theoretically there persists the danger of one inflicting harm unto another, it is knowledge of the importance for each of us to attain a state of truth and love that pushes us to protect and liberate those in suffering. For the moment I understand that becoming myself truly means fully embodying the particular aspect of God within *me*, I realize simultaneously that there is an aspect of God within *you*, which only you can become and fulfill, and thus the same for every person on this planet. Within us all is a piece of infinite uniqueness, a perfectly unique aspect of God, waiting to be encountered, accepted, manifested, and expressed, for us to *become*. And by the intercession and agency of Christ, it is through every one of us choosing to become the truth of ourselves in such a way that we realize a world of love.

All of us, together, living in expression of our truth within—this would be the full and complete actualization of love, of God.

All of us, in complete distinction and uniqueness, yet united fully with one another as we are united within ourselves. None higher, none lower. We are all the same; we are all unique.

All of us, unique waves but of the same sea. Unique leaves, but of the same tree. Unique rays of light, emanating from the same source. Unique points of attention, of the same infinity.

All of us, each unique and individual children of God, returning to the fullness of our inheritance upon redemption from the grasp of evil.

We, together, form the infinity. We become infinity—the face of God, the body of Christ.

We, together with Christ, become fully God and God fully us.

It is both, yet it is neither. It is multiplicity; it is infinity.

God is both; God is neither. God is more; God is the most.

Each of our lives thus hold cosmic significance. Without you—yes, *you*—we are all incomplete. I need you, just as you need me. We need each other, and without any of us, in very real terms, everyone is no one, and everything is nothing. We belong in a state of absolute interdependence, of *oneness*, in which we require as a fundamental necessity the consummation of all beings and aspects of the living universe, simply and only as themselves, in order to fully express and actualize God, and indeed the love of God, in our midst. To become *I*, that is, the truth of ourselves, therefore, is a matter of completion and incompletion—of life and death—not just for oneself, but for all and everything.

To be sure, this is not an attempt to coerce one into seeking and becoming the truth of oneself by a sort of peer pressure, claiming that one is liable to be the cause of suffering and loss for us all unless one becomes a certain way or adopts a given identity. Rather, what is being illustrated is a mode of being in which one freely chooses to accept and become as revealed by one's true nature, not because it is demanded of one by an outside entity or personal obligation, but out of a desire to be true to oneself and for the whole to desire truth from each individual. There is no coercion, no obligation, no force—simply and only desire.

But to say time and again, we do not choose who it is we truly are. Suggesting that because our true identity is derived from God—indeed, that it *is* God—we can therefore choose for it to be whatever we wish would be tantamount to asserting that it is we who create God and not God who creates and fashions us. Let us, therefore, be crystal clear: God and the truth are eternal, unchanging, and immutable; our only choice is to either discover and accept, or not. There are no exceptions, no middle ground or third way.

Towards such a reality, our reaction might be to lash out in defiance and to forcefully assert one's will against what we might perceive as the tyranny of God, in the form of this unchangeable nature within us that beckons us to become it. *Defiance 'til the death! Pride 'til I die!* So we might say, refusing acceptance of God and the truth as *I*, choosing instead to live and die by freedom in the form of our will alone, pure and unrefined.

Such an attitude, however, is to my mind a fallacy. For although God is most definitely our master—indeed, our Father—who has fashioned and bestowed an identity for us to become irrespective of our conscious choice, God is at the same time completely reliant on our freedom to become this person, which, to be sure, is who we really are. It is, to say again, the truth. God is thus our master, our dependent, and the truth of ourselves, all at once. Though one may cling to freedom simply for freedom's sake and "be free," it is at the same time a state of denial, an escape from what is the truth, and what one might perceive as the struggle between one's free will and an imposing, external God is simply a struggle between oneself and one's true identity, stemming from a refusal to accept and submit to the ultimate reality of the latter. Therefore, what may appear on the surface to be freedom and a display of strength and independence is, in fact, willfulness and conceit; to say further, insofar that such a disposition is not based on truth, it is a lie—a *sin* and thus evil.

It is the Devil.

For indeed, it must be remembered that the Devil uses any and all means to deceive and enslave us, to hide us from the knowledge of ourselves and then to inhibit the decision and process to become ourselves, thus united with God. Even this system that we live under, with all its machinery to keep us in a state of darkness and bondage, is but merely a tool for the Devil's ultimate aim of usurping the truth of God. When the time comes and the system as we see it today collapses and fades, this will by no means cease the opposition from the Devil. There will always be temptation—to stop thinking, to fixate on something, anything, other than the truth within us and the world we can build thereupon, to surrender to impositions and be controlled by that which brings death, to fall into ignorance. Waiting, lurking in the shadows, for the first and any opening of weakness, the Devil will watch.

The Devil is our adversary; it is Satan.

So, for the final time, then, to ask the question: Where is all this headed?

God loves for the sake of love, as the Alpha and Omega on our journey to exist as none but the truth of ourselves. The Devil hates us and seeks to scupper and impede at all costs the purpose of our lives as such. Both, it would seem, in perpetuity and for eternity.

It is a conflict, a war, of the greatest magnitude and consequence for us all, with our minds as the battleground and our *spirit* as the ultimate prize. The force of hatred is still very much apparent, the system and its pillars yet strong and imposing. But there are also signs everywhere, all around, of awakening, searching, and growth; of altruism, charity, creativity, expression, community, unity—of life and love.

I am the battleground for this war.
I am the one who chooses the victor.

The outcome is decided by me.

And the only thing that lies between the two—between life and death—is a choice.

All it takes is a choice.

Don't let it slip away.

Printed in Great Britain
by Amazon